Holy Sparks

Social Theory, Education and Religion

Philip Wexler

First published 1997 by
MACMILLAN PRESS LTD
Houndmills, Basingstoke, Hampshire RG21 6XS
and London
Companies and representatives
throughout the world

ISBN 0-333-69924-6

A catalogue record for this book is available from the British Library.

10 9 8 7 6 5 4 3 2 1
06 05 04 03 02 01 00 99 98 97

Book design by Milton Heiberg Studios

Printed in the United States of America by
Haddon Craftsmen
Scranton, PA

Because I have loved so deeply
Because I have loved so long,
God in his great compassion
Gave me the gift of song.

—Nina Simone

Contents

Acknowledgments

Many friends and colleagues helped, in innumerable and various ways, enable me to write this book. I want to thank especially: Ari Antikainen, Basil Bernstein, Catherine Casey, Malcolm Clarkson, Ivor Goodson, Laurie Kash, Joe Kincheloe, Lauren Langman, Johan Muller, William Pinar, Francois and Deborah Raoult, Eleanor Rosenfield, Alan Sadovnik, William A. Scandling, Naomi Schlagman, Arieh Simon, Richard Smith, Shirley Steinberg, Heinz Sunker, and Margaret Zaccone. Special thanks to Paul Stein for his careful and imaginative assistance in readying the manuscript for publication.

Michael Flamini, senior editor at St. Martin's, is an editor in the grand style, and I am lucky to work with him. The late Christopher Lasch offered intellectual stimulation, patient dialogue, and local political support over many years. He helped me to see the current crisis in deeper, civilizational terms and encouraged me to pursue what he referred to as my "religious sensibility." I miss him.

My family—Ilene, Michael, Ari, Helen and Ava—are my closest friends and partners; without them, nothing. This book is dedicated with love to my mother, Mindy Langsam, who has been a great teacher and exemplar for me, and to my grandmothers, Nechama Kimmel Braver and Anna Wexler. They carried the tradition through very hard times, from generation to generation.

—Philip Wexler
April 1996

Part One

Critique and Contextual Foundations

Chapter One

Revision: Social Theory, Education and Religion

Beyond Critical Theory and Postmodernism

Social analyses often represent unspoken drives and desires. Here, the drive of analysis is libidinal, energizing and procreative: to affirm life. Not simply to affirm the abstract value of life, but to affirm the actual capacity for human living, for sensory experience, intentionally regulated consciousness—indeed, for the happiness that we now call "optimal being." The capacity to be fully human.

Of course, this is the goal of virtually every ethic. Social science, however, has long claimed indifference to drives, desires, values and ethics. But sociology and history of knowledge, science and social science repeatedly have shown that seemingly indifferent knowledge is integral to particular forms of life, to beliefs and values, and to everyday cultural practices. Knowledge is not indifferent, only extracted from its roots and separated from its implications for ethics of being.

Critical social theory and postmodernism opposed the deracination and seeming indifference of social knowledge. Both have had a good run at opposing objectivism or essentialism in social science, in social theory and in education. And, I think, they both have failed. Critical social theory, when it was not arcane, sublimated its drive to reconnect theory with active social life by projecting its creative, transformative ethics of social being into an eschatology, an imagined ideal future. Postmodernism fused critical philosophy, linguistic and literary poststructuralism and popular aesthetics into a substitute for the transformative urge, only to see this fusion become a fetishized quietism, a stunned surrender to implosion and the diffusion of the present moment of being into reaggregated collections of mass cultural artifacts. Eschatology, diffusion, and temporal/spatial displaced projections away from any centered present are respectively the current tendencies of critical social theory and postmodernism, when they are not reduced to appearing as slogans in academic and mass cultural theory or as institutional totalitarianism in practice.

Postmodern critical theory—if one may dare to conflate these disparate traditions—did posit "difference" as a vantage point that could be used to revisit and alter the present. But, this difference, whether as "otherness" or as the transcendental direction of what is "entirely different," or "otherwise," remains empty, void of substantive definition except as a virtuous principle, or as an approval of conventional pluralism. The burning question of how to see things clearly and how to live the present differently is not answered, unless the character of the difference can be elaborated. If, for example, transcendence is the final point of difference, critique and transformation, then what is the site of that transcendence? And how does its specific character affect social understanding and life in the present? We want to go beyond an appreciation of the principle of a transcendental vantage point for criticism of the present in order to develop a more *systematic social understanding that works to transform the present toward optimal being*—a transformation that neither critical theory nor postmodern cultural theory has yet succeeded in effecting.

Theory and Culture

This interest in "theory," in social understanding, assumes that theory can be effective and that it is much closer to everyday life in the present than the historically legitimating distance of indifference has presented and institutionalized as academic social science.

Social theory is viewed here as growing out of everyday cultural practice, and as amplifying and rationalizing those practices, in much the same way as the earliest natural sciences began in the craft practices of navigators and folk healers. Changes in social theory, in this account, are not limited to either research accumulation or paradigm shifts coming from within the community of academic theory practitioners. Changes in systematic social understanding reverberate from less well articulated and broader changes in everyday culture and can feed back to amplify and redirect those changes.

The failure of critical theory and postmodernism, from this viewpoint, is not simply one of a scientific or analytical incompetence. Rather, it is a historical failing, a hermeneutical lag, a poor reading of cultural tendencies that becomes encapsulated and frozen during the necessary rationalization process of knowledge, but then assumes its own velocity, separated from cultural grounding as well as from collective aspirations and values. What forces us beyond critical theory and postmodernism is sociocultural change. We are urged on at once by the failure to realize desires for transformed being, and by the emergence of cultural "incipients" or new cultural elements with a different direction and language. Inertia or entropy in social theory is represented by our need to dismiss or incorporate cultural changes, even when they shatter prevailing paradigmatic assumptions. *Revision* is the antidote, the negative entropy.

Here, I take a different path. Instead of ignoring or explaining away what may seem anomalous, I take cultural divergences as new ground for social theory and as a redirection for the underlying critical project of transforming the present toward full human realization. Rather than accept "transcendence" as an abstract, general vantage point for social criticism, I try to enter into the substantive meaning of at least some views of the transcendental. Following this path requires a certain flexibility and openness toward currents of sociocultural change. It requires a willingness to revise paradigmatic assumptions by taking cultural change seriously.

The complaint of critical theory and postmodernism against objectivism and essentialism is grounded in a critique of a prevailing culture and form of life. The critique is about alienation in everyday life, about cultural monolithism, about economic exploitation, inequality and affliction, and the rationalization and commodification of everyday social life and subjective experience, the so-called colonization of the lifeworld. My interest is not simply an aesthetic analytical one in an intriguing interweaving of practical culture and social theory. Rather, I share the practical social criticism of class exploitation and inequality, patriarchal oppression, white racism, and the pervasive commodification of social relations and reification of individual consciousness. Now, however, I want to go far beyond critique—toward a simultaneous practical affirmation of the life force that is socially being destroyed and to the articulation of a *positive,* alternative social theory.

The interest in the relation between social theory, cultural change and a transcendental or religious basis for critique is not hypothetical. I would assert that, increasingly, alongside pervasive commodification, rationalization, and destruction in everyday social life, there are now cultural alternatives. Moving against—but existing simultaneously with—commodification, there are multiple expressions of what I broadly call a "religious" interest, a common press toward the *resacralization of everyday life.* As a critical social theorist, I know sadly how interest in the sacred works as a diversion and distraction from attention to and rectification of systematic, socially generated suffering and how interest in the sacred is incorporated into the commodity process, offering many new product-lines for profit. I know how when it is not included in the production and consumption process, its seeming alterity or deep difference from the mundane has been murderously expressed in collective cultic and fundamentalist forms. I was born during the Holocaust and grew up during the years of the Gulag and saw the expressions these cultic forms took. Even so I harbor an optimism toward the positive power of the sacred. Just as Max Weber juxtaposed charisma to rationalization, I suggest that resacralization opposes commodification. Resacralization can be an *historically transformative, creative cultural force.*

I want to do more than simply suggest that along with the commodification of social life that has been identified, analyzed and criticized for so many years, there is also a resacralization that presents a dangerous and narrow, but potentially fertile, opening for sociocultural change toward more creative and life-affirming social relations. For, if social theory is integral to culture, then with changing cultural gestalts, epistemes, or mentalities, theory can also be revised, provided there is a willingness to suspend the practiced claims of indifference and of cultural superordination and epistemological privilege. With that surrender comes the possibility of theorizing from within the changed culture. What I suggest in this book is a *resacralization of social theory.*

Sociocultural Change

The sociocultural changes occurring are complex and multiform. Economic rationalization and commodification intensify and penetrate all public social institutions. While our interest in education is much wider and deeper than the issue of schooling, the school institution is a key site for the intensification and, indeed, the elaboration of rationalizing processes. I continue to use the term "corporatism" to index these changes in education because I want to draw attention not only to the rationalization and commodification of the social relations of schooling, but also to the changing structures of institutional control and regulation, "governance" in a social sense. David Harvey (1989) argued persuasively about the way in which changes in production, to a post-Fordist regime, are aligned with the cultural changes called postmodernism. I would emphasize, even more than Harvey does, the need to further underline and empirically study the shifts in social-individual identity dynamics and subjectivity that also occur during this time.

Education—both narrowly and broadly defined—is the area I focus on for analyzing sociocultural changes, and so I begin a description of institutional change in education, and then at the level of individual identities. Postmodern culture is not only part of the same social regime, as Harvey argues, but also a failed potential alternative to rationalizing modernity. Postmodernism, notwithstanding such engaging descriptions as that of Celeste Olalquiaga (1992), does not work sufficiently as a mass cultural practice, whatever its successes in the academy. It is the cultural failure of a postmodern alternative that opens the way for the reassertion of premodern religious-sounding cosmologies under the rubric of "new age."

Most professional social analysts err in dismissing new age culture as an extension of advertising. I may err on the other side, seeking harbingers of a new civilization in what may simply turn out to be the mass subjective aspect of postmodern consumerism, after all. Still, from the revivalism of twelve-step methods in psychotherapy, to my neighbors' worship of various goddesses and to *Time* magazine's discovery that more than two thirds of all Americans believe in angels, to the gnosticism of literary critics such as Harold Bloom (1992) and even to the ascendance of yoga over aerobics fitness classes, there is unavoidable but scattered evidence of a commonality in a plethora of disparate changes in cultural practices. Wade Roof (1993) sees these commonalities in his studies of the spiritual quests of the baby-boom generation. The common theme is resacralization, *the return of cultural practices of the sacred to everyday social life,* simultaneous with the continuing rationalization and commodification of profane mundanity.

Social Theory

The link between new age culture and a revision of social theory is not direct. While I take new age culture seriously as a topic of analysis, it is not the transparent resource for a transcendental critical social theory. Rather, I understand the new age cultural expressions as a shift in popular episteme, or, as Pitirim Sorokin would have put it, much earlier, the expression of a new cultural premise or assumption. Specifically, Sorokin's (1957) view of sociocultural dynamics is constructed on the grand scale, predicting a painful decline of the materialist sensate culture to be followed either by its opposite, a religious ideational culture, or by an intermediate rationalist idealist culture.

If I follow Sorokin in seeing a deeper, long-term cultural evolution at work in these changes, I do not follow him in the conceit of having surpassed classical sociology. Instead, I return, with a Bloom-like revisionary attitude, to the sociological theory canon, casting major theorists as precursors, not to my own view, but to what I believe will become a very different foundation and vocabulary in social understanding—one based in a number of the sacred traditions that a disenchanted, modernist sociology abandoned, at least in its conventional, surface presentation. So, I revise, looking for subtexts and minor chords, for precursors and forgotten figures, in order to show that theorizing society from within the sacred is neither merely a new age derivative nor a faddish fabrication.

On the contrary, while I suggest that the sacralization of social theory is facilitated by historically changed cultural conditions—new age culture—rather than de novo by theoretical innovations, I also note that it is continuous with critical traditions of modern European social analyses. Yet, even this continuity with the contemporary interest in the sacred aspect of social life is in itself an insufficient resource for the elaboration and articulation of an alternative critical social theory. Resacralization in culture and theory only opens the gate for revision. Revision will have to go farther afield than an appropriative misreading of the sociological mainstream tradition.

Finding antecedents for new age and religious emphases and aspirations in the tradition of indifferent social science is a revision, even a misprision, in the interests of creation, or as Bloom would have it, psychoanalytically: " a deliberately perverse misreading, whose purpose is to clear away the precursor so as to open a space for oneself" (1982:64). The desire for cultural revision, for identity, leads to tradition in social theory and not to an abstract mimesis of new age culture in the domain of critical social theory. But, identification and bonding with secular sociological traditions is not adequately demarcating. Such a revision does not open enough space for a greater autonomy from even the critical social theory tradition. The reason for that is ultimately (following, but then deviating from Weber) because sociology, as a modern project, is a secularization—like much of modern culture—of innerworldly, ascetic Protestantism. Arthur Vidich and Stanford Lyman (1986) make the same secularization case, in historic detail, for American sociology.

If the mainstream of social theory is a secularization of religious interests, and if the main tendency in that secularization was a translation or recontextualization of ascetic Protestantism into secular sociology, then any effort to read social theory backward—through new age culture, to reenchantment and resacralization—ought to at least try to appropriate, and revise, a much wider sample of sacred belief. I do not do all of that here. Joel Kovel (1991) has attempted to read through radical social theory to Christianity, and Michael Lowy (1992) has tried to connect critical German sociology to mainstream Jewish belief. I do attempt a similar work, and for example, I recontextualize Basil Bernstein's (1990) sociology of education, through Emile Durkheim, to rabbinic Judaism. But, my view of the connection between new age culture, including the hypothesis of a deeper cultural shift and a religious or "ideational" culture is that the return to the premodern core civilizational religions of Judaism, Islam, Christianity, Buddhism and Hinduism proceeds by way of rediscovery and representation—first, of their esoteric or mystical traditions (Merkur, 1993), since these are more easily assimilable to new age cultural themes, and then later, in a deeper return to the ancient traditions.

The development of social theory, outward from the core of sacred belief to a secularized sociology (which leads ultimately [Coleman, 1993] to the rational reconstruction not only of society, but also of social theory) is reversed—stepwise—in the resacralization process.

At each place in the reverse spiral, it is possible to revise, recontextualize, amplify and articulate sacred belief into systematic social understanding or explanation. So, for example, one could derive social explanation from mass new age culture, from more traditional—though esoteric, or mystical—aspects of civilizational religions, or from the classical, mainstream religious formulations. One can imagine then subsequent reversals of the reverse spiral, with new forms of secularization and rationalization. Social and cultural theory construction becomes an historically contingent revision within the dynamic spiral of secularization and sacralization.

I enter into this dynamic interplay with a dissent from postmodernism as a cultural theory. I try to show, as an example, how efforts—like Ian Hunter's (1994)—to supplant a critical social approach to education with a poststructuralist theory and postmodern attitude, are inadequate to the present moment. Instead, I see new age culture as successor to postmodernism and as evidence of a more fundamental cultural-civilizational change toward religious culture. Given the assumption of the integral connection between culture and social theory, this may appear as doing sociology religiously. I do start from resacralized concepts, but then try to build systematic social understanding from there, rather than from the secularized critical and postmodern theories, which are being surpassed in historical cultural practice.

Once the resacralization in theory and culture is reviewed and the precursors and subtexts for a religious sociology uncovered, I make a beginning toward an understanding of society and education on a new foundation, which represents a midpoint between new age culture and classical religion. While there is some flirtation with Taoism and Yoga, my main focus of elaboration of social theory and application to education is in Jewish esotericism. I start there because while the revisionary process is a revolutionary and subversive one, supplanting the authorial father, it is also a creatively receptive one, searching for the father's mother, the grandmother. In Judaism, spirituality and mysticism have been, at least since the early modern period, the less public figure, the silenced partner, the mother to fatherly rationalism, legalism, and rabbinism. Revision means also reestablishment of tradition beyond its most recent representation. It is a cultural creation of love as well as of anger and, beyond rejection of the preeminent precursor, also an acceptance of the precursor's matrilineage. Revision is a transgenerational process. In Judaism, this means, following Martin Buber, a swerve past rationalist rabbinism toward an existential mysticism.

I present this path only as the example closest to me. My expectation is that it is an instance of a multilineal vision, and that others will pursue the resacralization of social understanding in quite other traditions. Here, there is merely a clumsy beginning toward what must only be called a Jewish mystical sociology. This is less bizarre than it seems, once one considers the specifics of Max Weber's effort to theorize a way out of the "iron cage" (1958) of modernity. It may be understood, along with analysis of eroticism and aesthetics, as just another sphere in his panoply of alternative routes away from the limitations of a culture of secularized ascetic Protestantism. This beginning represents a possibility that he located logically and categorically, but left, largely, socially and culturally empty: *innerworldly mysticism*. I argue that innerworldly mysticism is the deeper cultural meaning of the new age—a trajectory from innerworldly asceticism to innerworldly mysticism (and not simply world-fleeing). Then, I try to rationalize, if not secularize, this orientation in an incipient social dynamics—as if to take seriously Durkheim's possibility of a "mystic mechanics" of society.

This approach to social life is then directed particularly toward understanding education in society as an important institutional site of social interaction and a place of subjectivity as well as an example of cultural change and shifts in social theory, after the twilight of critical sociology and postmodernism.

Education

The focus on education arises here for several reasons. First, my own earliest and continuing work has been to describe historical changes in culture as at least the background assumptions, following Alvin Gouldner (1970), for paradigmatic changes in social theorizing about education. *The Sociology of Education: Beyond Equality* (1976), for example, was an attempt to show that the emergence of what later became known as a "new sociology of education" was integral to American political and social movements and cultural history. *Social Analysis of Education* (1987) situated poststructuralism within postindustrialism.

In both instances, changes in sociology of education involved altered basic assumptions, which followed changes in general social theory and culture. Following along this line, the current effort is to anticipate new directions in the field of sociological—and more broadly, social theoretic—analyses of education, by constructing social theory outward from cultural movements.

Second, the more conventionally empirical aspect of my work repeatedly has emphasized research in schools as a primary way in which to study the transformation and differentiation of individual social identities. In studies of both Israeli and American high schools, what Basil Bernstein emphasized in the sociology of education as the macro-micro linkage was an attention directed toward describing how sociocultural changes work through educational institutions to change and differentiate individual identities in socially patterned ways. I carry some of this work forward in this book in order to show how the most recent institutional changes in schools can be related to social identity processes.

My hope is that this book works simultaneously at a number of levels. One level is to understand educational change institutionally—within corporatism and postmodernism—while drawing implications for identity. Secondly, given my emphasis on subjectivity as crucial for sociocultural change, I want to place self or identity changes—the "transformation from within"—that occur in and out of school as central to sociocultural change. The implications of new age culture for educational practice are just now beginning to be drawn, against the background of an almost overwhelming rationalization of knowledge, learning and teaching, in a purely technical, instrumental direction. The new age emphasis on the integration of body-mind-energy, a social metaphysic of expansive presence in the here and now, is the antithetical curriculum to the performance-based petrification and containment of the soul in corporatist, Toyota-production style schooling.

This points to the third reason for highlighting education. One point of the New Left departure during the sixties and seventies was not only to emphasize personal identity politics, but also to view collective consciousness, starting with the traditional concept of class consciousness, as a fundamental political and analytical interest. Education, construed broadly, well beyond schooling, is about the social transformation of consciousness. And, "consciousness" is itself construed broadly, for it includes recognition of unconsciousness and the relevance of depth and cognitive psychologies for understanding the individual subject of cultural change and social transformation. My interest in education is simultaneously an interest in a transformative social psychology. As I did in the field of sociology of education, I have worked that interest through critical and postmodern tendencies (Wexler, 1983; 1992). A thread of questioning running through this book revolves around what a resacralized culture and social theory implies for analysis of social interaction and the self.

Fourth, interest in a theory of social interaction, of self and consciousness moves the focus of sociology of education beyond the institutional and cultural level to approach *interaction* in education. Sociologists of education have regrettably, but perhaps wisely, kept generally aloof from basic questions of teaching and learning. Wisely, because the enormous quantity of educational and psychological research and philosophical discourse on these topics seems remarkably inconclusive within the academic community and widely ignored or disparaged among educators outside of it. The theoretical direction toward transformative social interaction is almost the core of education, usually understood as teaching and learning; the question is unavoidable. Tentatively, I try to aim the resacralized redirection of social theory and education toward this critical, but complex question of teaching and learning.

Finally, my interest in education is mundane and practical. For almost a decade, as a professor and dean in a school of education, I have worked within the complex social movement for educational change, or reform, so-called. This work anchors transcendental interests in practical educational politics, across institutional sectors. Despite the importance of cultural process and social theory, I emphasize that the original interest in all of these questions, including sociology of education, is a practical, individual and transformative, or even revolutionary one.

That question is about how educational practice and social theory can work to overcome the alienation experienced in everyday life: the absence of adequate meaning, control, awareness and fullness of experience. It is worth remembering that the cultural movements of the 1960s were not only political, in the sense of seeking social empowerment—movements that later became academically expressed by emphasis on class, race and gender in the social study of education. The coterminous *cultural* aspect of this movement was in the desire for another form of life, inclusive and beyond political equality, that empowered a different way of being in the world.

In a sense, both critical social theory and postmodernism carried out the criticism of society, education, language, identity and consciousness that grew from that transformative drive. Contemporary cultural movements, I believe, stem from the same impulse. What is now different is the deployment of tacit strategies of transcendence and the resacralization movements in culture and theory that flow out from it.

Now, "religion" takes the transformative place held historically by education. If religion once was superseded by education as the social process of shaping individuals ("bildungsprozess") (Sunker, 1994), it now has reappeared on the cultural horizon with the potential of a collectively transformative social practice. Simultaneously, education is rationalized by corporatist practice under the banner of "high performance" and dissipated in postmodern theories that no longer profess a desire to transform consciousness. This is the place that we now want to explore and to integrate with the preceding counteralienating, transformative interests of social theory and education.

Religion

The foundation of social theory in religion is not a new age phenomenon. Against the textbook positivist interpretations, I read Durkheim and Weber as deeply committed to the view of religion as the primal social activity and as the underlying basis both of stable social meaning and of social change. Durkheim (1960:350) wrote of religious phenomena as "the germ from which all others . . . are derived." Among Weber's complaints against modernity was that the fundamental significance of religion for understanding culture and history was being missed (1958). Religion, as charisma, was the revolutionary force of history. And religion, despite its false leads, was still the surest way out of the iron cage of petrified life in the modern era.

My revision goes beyond underlining the religious and spiritual understandings and commitments of the precursors of sociological theory. The Romantic tradition, especially among the left psychoanalysts, Norman Brown, Wilhelm Reich and Erich Fromm, is deeply and openly intertwined with religious theories and aspirations. Perhaps Fromm (1966) took those furthest, in his attempt to translate social radicalism back to the Old Testament. In Fromm, the critical theory focus on alienation joins the psychoanalytic emphasis on libido or life force ("chayiut," or vitality in terms of the esoteric Judaism) with a religious equation of alienation and Old Testament idolatry. Ultimately, it is desire for the dealienated state, for what I have called the fully human or optimal being, that leads Fromm (1994) to cultural practices for the transformation of consciousness, which he referred to as "arts of being." These arts concretize his ideal of a "city of being" and are transparently spiritual practices (1976).

The confluence then of social theory, transformative practice (education, construed broadly) and religious traditions is not novel. What has changed, as Fromm predicted (1976), is that with mass movements for resacralization, pre-Enlightenment cosmologies come to function at a mass social level simultaneously as ethics of being and as folk social psychological theories. In addition to describing this change, what I want to do is create social theory from within it, amplifying, articulating, revising, and feeding back into a dual cycle or loop of practice and theory and secularization and sacralization. I want to go beyond Romanticism, even in its resacralized appearance.

Buber may be the inappropriate vehicle for this connection of social theory, education and religion. His path was strongly Romantic, originating in German philosophy of culture (Mendes-Flohr, 1989). Yet, Buber is a bridge, going even further afield from the West European Enlightenment than the socialist psychoanalyst Fromm. Buber is a bridge to the premodern social thought and practice of Jewish pietism, "chasidism," and also to an existential mysticism that reaches on one side toward Taoism, Buddhism and Yoga, and on the other, to a libertarian communalism that is based in a transformative theory of social interaction: the intersubjective communion of I and Thou.

This communion is an alternative to the rationalized performance of Toyota-type schooling. The educational application of Buber's dialogism and communalism had been tried in the autonomous youth villages of prestate Israel. In fact, when I studied this form of social education (Wexler, 1972), the Israeli educator Arieh Simon invited me to live in the house of Siegfried Lehmann, his mentor and the village founder. Lehman was a student and admirer of Buber; his preserved living room, amidst an agricultural school, eerily displayed German intellectual cultural artifacts of the 1920s, including an inscribed photo from Buber to a "fighter for education."

Despite this early personal affinity, Buber is only the best known modern representative of Jewish mysticism. The door that he opens leads to the canonical scholarship of Gershom Scholem, and the more recent work in Kabbalah of Moshe Idel, Adin Steinsaltz, Areh Kaplan and Allen Afterman. In their work, beyond Buber's inspired, poetic plea to hallow everyday social relations, can be found a rich storehouse of systematic conceptualizations and theories of "mystic mechanics" that I begin to recontextualize and interpret from a social analytic viewpoint.

What the voyage through new age culture finally accomplishes is the *replenishment of the cultural resources* for a renewal of social theory, which, in turn, can be elaborated as a new foundation for education—albeit in a language that alternates between modern social theory interests and premodern, transcendental mystical cosmologies. Postmodern valuation of hybridization, pastiche, mélange and blurring legitimates its succession by efforts to revise and reconceptualize ancient dynamics in light of the present. Critical theory comes full circle, to an admission of the unequivocal necessity of tradition and traditional theory.

With suitable irony, however, this is a tradition that does not value replication, but defines itself, as Scholem (1971) argues, as *incessant revision,* creatively interpretive commentary, and cultural revolution on the basis of an archetypal revelation. This is a charisma in history that evaporates any linear, progressive notion of time and instead offers ritual cycles that function to erase the difference between past, present and future. Franz Rosenzweigi in Nathan Glatzer (1953) and Emmanuel Levinas (1990, 1994) seize this ritual production of infinitude, as a way out of European philosophies of time and being and, for Levinas (1994), as a distancing from their putative termination in the Holocaust. Such a model of theoretical revision demands a renewal of life in social practice, an intentionality of transformative action in everyday interchange, that I understand as education.

Through a rereading of the sociological canon of Durkheim and Weber, Romantic social psychology, and the attempt to theoretically bolster popular new age notions of "energy," the drive against alienation and toward optimal being leads first to the edges of social theory with Buber and Fromm and then over the border, to sacred theories of social/self dynamics. Finally, it leads toward the resecularization of religious theory, in the simultaneous desire for explanation and transformation that characterizes not only critical social theory, but also any viable culture.

Perhaps sacrilegiously, I struggle not only to rekindle the "holy sparks" of light and energy remaining from the primal creative destruction (sparks that, according to the kabbalistic narrative of universal beginning, remain indwelling worldly places for creativity). I also struggle to recollect such sparks in the interests of a vivifying social theory and socioeducational practice. The struggle may be a long and circuitous route for social renewal, but it is the path that new age culture opens for us—after the salutary destruction and emptying of postmodernism—in looking toward a greater horizon of social knowledge.

Renaissance

In the long run, revivification through resacralization is the path of cultural, theoretical and educational renaissance. This path works outward, from, as Buber (3:139) wrote of education, the "holy spark crossing the gap" to an individual process of resubjectification and a collective one of resymbolization. What the new age aura represents is the initial effort to counteract what Weber (1958) referred to as the "mechanical petrification" of modernity with an instantaneous energy.

The quest for immediacy makes the vivifying, libidinal drive vulnerable to use and incorporation in the global commodity-producing apparatus and turns the search for an ethic of being into a series of postindustrially packaged addictions: *the culture of death,* superficially and aesthetically coated to conceal its effects. As Weber understood, the work of intellectuals is to sublimate or translate the drive for salvation into ideas. Only then does it offer the possibility of a new ethos, or systematic, rational theory and practice of social life. Failure to rationally articulate, encouraged both by mysticism and commodity culture, feeds cultural stasis and aborts the rebirth of a vital culture. The value of innerworldly mysticism is not in a permanent silence, an antieducational nontransmissibility, but in its recollection and recentering of presently socially petrified energies. Stopping with the experienced silence fuels only narcissism, which boosts the addictive psychology of the commodity apparatus and bloats its operators.

Revision demands not only primordial memories of archetypal revelation, but rational interpretation, commentary and educative communication, under social conditions of mutuality and reciprocity. The educational question becomes ever more central in this renaissance scenario. For me, any question of "undistorted speech" (Habermas, 1987) is not only a cognitive or moral question, but also a libidinal one, an energizing question. It is an issue of *social* desire, not of privatized implosion, libidinal or informational. Neither a universal nor a particularist, but an entirely social solution is called for—one in which there is interaction between sacred generativity; communicative, educational hermeneutics; and unimpeded individual flows of energy that may derive from natural or transcendental sources, but appear in the immediate relations between self and society.

In this book, I do not complete this historical scenario. But, I do hope to articulate a cultural and social theoretic path from the present moment, in order to show how social theory, education and religion are inevitably implicated in our work.

Chapter Two

Sociocultural Foundations

Education and Sociology in Cultural Change

I see sociocultural changes being identified and questioned in disparate areas: in academic discussions about postmodernism; in popular cultural expressions of new age resacralization; in a changing sociology and in the shifting premises and directions of sociology of education. Changes occur concretely in social institutions, and I begin by describing the current "restructuring" or "reform" movement in education as part of a wider process of social structural rationalization, instrumentalization and corporatism.

Identity and cultural dynamics are not simple extensions of these structural processes. Often, they are counterpoints. Nor are identity processes uniform in all schools, representing some universal postmodern self-dissolution. Rather, processes of self-redefinition are defenses against both the rationalizing corporatism of school reform and the increasingly empty direction of postmodern fragmentation. These processes are socially variable, by class, gender and race. Cultural movements also promise to become counterpoints and I suggest that postmodernism is a failed alternative to modern, rational corporatism, simply because it is not different enough.

The search for a cultural foundation for a different form of life leads first to a critique of postmodernism and then to a reading of recent sociology as both cultural movement and artifact. Sociology is also a site for exploring first charisma and then resacralization, both as alternatives to postmodern forms of educational rationalization and as means of demonstrating how the sociocultural foundations of ascetic Protestantism become unraveled within a new age culture.

Recent cultural history is even more clearly represented in the sub-field of sociology of education. More closely integrated with practice and more vulnerable to cultural shifts, the recent progress of the sociology of education accurately reflects the recent path of movement from critical sociology, with its explicit political interests, to the aestheticization of imported postmodern theory and onward to an emergent religious interest. My interest is not only to provide empirical correction, but also to be socially critical and, finally, to suggest a historical transcendence toward a utopia of sorts.

There is a powerful movement to transform the social, cultural and psychological organization of educational institutions. Despite the ostensibly Marxist attention to education, with a few exceptions, there has been remarkably little analytical description of the social movement in education that I referred to almost a decade ago as a corporatist reorganization.

A great deal has happened since then, and the earlier emphasis on a privatization process that was combined with moral attacks on the "secular humanism" of school culture captured only the most salient, but I think not the most enduring, aspects of the continuing social reorganization of education. It is rather the progressive, liberal platform of educational reform and "restructuring" that represents a partnership of the state, business corporations, and significant groups of educational professionals that is effecting change in the infrastructure and, ultimately, the very meaning of education.

During the moment of a new corporatist structural reorganization and redefinition of education, there is an everyday, socially differentiated struggle for identity among students who, in corporatist language, are referred to as the "workers of the school." The everyday social existence of youths in schools is a concrete instance of the decentering, lack and absence that is usually presented in a textual register in postmodern discourse about "the subject." Socially oriented postmodernism that reaches beyond textualism speaks in very general terms about macrosocial trends like "implosion," rather than describing the specific meanings of either poststructuralism as a theory, or postmodernism as a form of life in the institutions within which "the subject" acts, disappears or is "decentered."

Articulations of identity in a postmodern world presume the triumph of consumption as the lead social activity. Instead, we have studied everyday school life in different social strata and have tried to describe not a textual, but an institutional postmodernism in which there are socially differentiated "lacks." These absences are experienced by youths, who struggle with and against them, in their efforts to establish distinguishable identities—to become somebody.

The long-term effect of the social reorganization and institutional emptying may, I think, realize postmodern predictions about the end of grand narratives, collapse of the referentials and death of the subject, or critical theory's projections about the closing of the universe of discourse and the reduction of autonomous spheres of social life to one dimension. More likely, the restructuring will combine the microflexibility of classroom production, the macrointegration of social regulation, and the interlocking networks of control to produce discipline and legitimation.

The moral conservatism that appears still relevant in educational censorship seems an unlikely candidate for the type of resocialization required by a new, flexible, performance-oriented schooling. This moral conservatism may be appropriate for ideologies of nostalgia, but it is less appropriate for education in the electronic age. The need for remoralization poses questions of meaning against the current of new corporatist, performance-driven, flattening and institutionally emptying desocialization. This contradiction between techno-performance cultural destruction and the need for culture is the transformative site in education.

New Corporatism in Education

The first wave of corporatism in education combined an effort to destroy the civic culture of republicanism in school, which the then so-called moral majority movement referred to as secular humanism, with both commodification and privatization of public schooling (Wexler and Grabiner, 1985). The agency of rationalization was a series of business/education voluntarist partnerships. While the arrangements were largely local, we did see them in light of Leo Panitch's definition of corporatism:

> a political structure within advanced capitalism which integrates organized socioeconomic producer groups through a system of

> representation and cooperative mutual interaction at the leadership level and of mobilization and social control at the mass level.(1977:66)

The vocabulary of change was one of educational accountability, educational competency, and school efficiency. Now, the language has changed, and with it the adopt-a-school format of friendly local business assistance for school improvement has become an increasingly integrated national corporatist network promoting new national standards through "break the mold" schools. The mold to be broken is the bureaucratic factory school, and change in the language of educational reform underlines the fact that we have moved well beyond corporatist school improvement to the establishment of education as both more closely linked to economic production organization and as a social form directly analogous to new modes of production.

The so-called new American school (and this is the model whether emanating directly from the New American Schools Development Corporation or from the separate statewide initiatives that are increasingly linked by national networks unified under the aegis of educational issues, particularly those of standardization of outcomes or the educational product and its measurement or quality control) is a "Toyota school" (Schmoker, 1992:23). It is seen as a high-performance school that is run by new-collar leaders who design hands-on, real-life, team-organized learning of new skills for a restructured workplace:

> The failure of our industrial managers to persuade more workers to design and build quality products is no different from the failure of teachers (the managers of students) to persuade more students to do quality schoolwork. (Glasser,1992:32)

There is no longer any pretense of an organized public institutional mediation between education and economic production. From the school-to-work transition to the redefinition of educational knowledge and, finally, to the subject of schooling (the student), education is to be reorganized both to mirror restructured workplaces as organizations and to match them by a smoother flow and transfer of the product, from student to worker. New corporatism is simultaneously the vehicle and the expression of an increasingly elite organized, mass-mobilized, national social movement to create a postindustrial, post-Fordist educational apparatus that will match the economic shift to a new regime of capital accumulation.

The language of education is the language of restructured work. Individual schools, school systems, states, and the nation's "America 2000" all need "vision statements." The crisis of productivity (Ray and Mickelson, 1989) and global economic competition which induces the creation of the restructured workplace (and as a corollary, the restructured school), requires benchmarked, national, and eventually computer-networked assessments of the products of "this new model of work, organization and management." Educational leaders and teachers are team leaders and "vendors of schooling" as a "client driven," "worklife derived commodity." The crisis of education is recast as a "design problem."

There are many examples of new national networks of elite leaders and the design of educational reform along the lines of the "restructuring model." These newer networks are different in direction and composition from the moral-critiques and curriculum-censorship movement, despite the salience of continuated advocacy of the moral majority line. The possibility of public financing of private education under the banner of individual choice remains on the agenda; it is complemented by publicity for national chains of privately owned schools, and the encouragement of deregulated charter schools. However the main tendency in school reform is to restructure public schools to be like restructured workplaces so that they will be high-performance organizations producing measurably high-quality learning outcomes that will enable high-skill jobs to be competitively accomplished by new-collar American workers in the global marketplace.

Corporatist social forms include not only the elite functional representation that appears in the emergent national educational restructuring networks, but also mass mobilization. Increasingly entire communities are encouraged to join expanded coalitions. Parents are organized in tandem to work for reform under the slogan of parental involvement. At a recent "parental involvement summit," the Executive Director of the National Committee for Citizens in Education, William Rioux, called the meeting an historic occasion. He said:

> "For me, when 23 organizations willfully and openly acknowledge the role of parents in the academic success of their children and in the success of schools overall all, that's a benchmark." (Sommerfield,1992:1)

Full community mobilization to restructure public schooling to the new model is an essential and growing part of the new corporatism in education.

The reorganization of educational control through the establishment of interlocking networks may increase the centralization of the design function at the same time that the design itself calls for a greater degree of innovative, customized and, above all, flexible social organization and school culture. Even the standardization that the main restructuring networks propose, test and implement is justified on the ground that it will provide flexibility. In a public discussion of nationally standardized testing, Marc Tucker, a director of the New Standards Project, explains:

> Lastly, we determined that such a system must be flexible. I have already cited one example: many exams, one standard. There is another more subtle way in which flexibility is essential . . . the score depends on their cumulative accomplishments over time. . . . In the first instance we expect those tasks to be centrally designed. But over time, we want them to be largely designed by classroom teachers for their own use, in their own schools, in their own classrooms. That's flexibility. That will be a world in which the teachers have internalized the standards. . . . (Tucker, 1992:4)

The other director of the project, Lauren Resnick, indicates that a new standard is for a new type of knowledge, one that is especially not "the assembly-line version of knowledge." And in another plan for school restructuring, the New Visions Schools Project, the former New York City schools' chancellor described the effort to create a less impersonal setting in experimental theme-oriented schools. "In contrast, the new schools are to be more 'flexible'," the chancellor said. (Bradley, 1992a:5).

The precise content of the flexible, anti-assembly-line knowledge in schools is not, however, easily agreed upon. Some states, like Maine, have had commission reports redefining the traditional curriculum into core learning that will achieve "151 goals for student learning." The four organizing areas of knowledge are: communication, personal and global stewardship, reasoning and problem solving, and the human record (Viadero,1992:21). The most widely discussed new curriculum is the Labor Department's commission report of the

Secretary's Commission on Achieving Necessary Skills (SCANS). The report, "Learning a Living: A Blueprint for High Performance," calls for an approach that sounds like the Toyota school: teamwork, collaborative learning, and a set of changes in teacher education and professional development. The new pedagogical skills that teachers need are:

> to teach in context and to develop active, collaborative learning environments; to learn new instructional management skills and use new instructional technologies that support new ways of interacting with students; and to gain experience with the principles of high performance as applied in restructured workplaces. (Harp,1992:10)

The commission described necessary knowledge for students as five competency areas:

> defined as the productive use of resourses, interpersonal skills, information systems and technology-built on a foundation of basic thinking skills and well-developed personal qualities.(Harp,1992:10)

The main point of the report, however, is that there must be a *translation* of work skills into the academic curriculum—a redefinition defined as the productive use of resources, of the curriculum as high-performance workplace—relevant skills, which are taught in "the context of real life situations and real problems." Arlene Penfield, president of the National School Boards Association, dissented that: "The report, for instance, goes too far in recommending that writing be reoriented from an 'academic' to a 'real world focus'" (Harp,1992:10). On the other hand, Albert Shanker, president of the American Federation of Teachers, observed that the report's recommendations come "not one moment too soon."

New knowledge of the new corporatism is, at least in a formal sense, the culture of the school (the informal, actual culture of the school is the social interaction of the students, which I describe in the next section). The attempt by David Harvey (1989) and others (Aronowitz, 1981; Wexler, 1987) to explicate the integral connection between the changing organization of production—from Fordism to a regime of flexible accumulation—and the culture of postmodernism is paralleled by the even more explicit tie between the restructured workplace (flexible accumulation) and the restructured, high-performance school.

The new knowledge or culture is, in the educational sector, expressly tied to the newly restructured workplace as a "translation" of "real-life" skills to academic curriculum. It represents a shift "from an 'academic' to a 'real world focus'." For those worried about the excessive narrowing of school knowledge to new workplace skills, there is reassurance that traditional disciplines such as history will also be included. Significantly, all social studies or sciences are absent from such a curriculum, represented only by history, "the human record." This absence of the social in knowledge or formal culture is particularly important, I think, given our findings about the alteration in the character of the informal culture of social interaction. There, our most general finding is that there is a practical deconstruction of the social, and that what is absent or lacking from the class-differentiated social text of schools are the specific central elements that constitute sociality—interaction, society and self.

The key to the new knowledge is that it redefines meaning and subjectivity. The fusion of spheres that new knowledge represents is a redefinition of knowing that places knowledge on a plane of high performance. The view of knowledge as a process of translation and standardization, with innovation and flexibility occurring within the controlled, structured standard, reduces the level of the agency of knowing to the level of a hands-on task, or more generally, to a horizontal level of knowledge (in Harvey's postmodern terms, to a flat, spatial performance that compresses knowledge into immediacy and contracts temporal depth into the moment "just in time"). The new knowledge makes knowing superficial. It removes both the cultural resources and the practice of any intellectual depth. Knowledge must now be task related, rather than autonomous and critical. In this sense, what we see in the new knowledge of schooling and in its formal culture is the concrete institutional example of the superficiality that postmodernism values as the new culture, generally. Both are cultures that deny depth, conscience, consciousness and unconsciousness in knowledge.

I call this "techno-surfacing," to differentiate it from a consumption-oriented superficiality or the decentering, diffusing, antinarrative pastiche eclecticism of genre- and domain-fused postmodern culture. What is further important about this one-dimensionalizing, or desocializing, of knowledge/culture is that it is not rooted in the spectacular culture of mass consumption. Instead, it displays, at an institutional level removed from the direct reorganization of economic production, how the redefinition of culture is mediated institutionally between production and culture in the educational sector. Education is not simply any institutional mediation. It is one of the primary self- or subject-formative institutions. Its techno-surfacing and de-socialization is directly relevant for identity formation.

Our current studies of high schools are present-day studies conducted between the collapse of the bureaucratic, assembly-line, model school and the design of a new school model for a regime of flexible accumulation. This redesign is being effected as redefinition and techno-surfacing in the educational, production-extended sphere displayed by postmodern accounts. This technical, instrumental redesign will also require remoralization. This will, in turn, reopen the cultural question and encourage cultural reconstruction as important public/private, corporatist work. Although such a "new culture" is designed to shore up institutional articulations of the new production regime, the drive toward cultural creation will be reignited within it. At that point, it will become possible for an alternative model to inscribe its "vision statement" onto history. The middle-run desocialization and the long-run potentially transformative contradiction between culturally reconstructive *regulation and a new cultural alternative are the themes of the next two sections.

Identity and Institution*

The student/subject result of high-performance new knowledge and a performative, "real-world" rather than academic focus is completed by an emergent attention to promoting healthy lifestyles. The noncognitive, intersubjective world through which identity is formed interactively is rendered superficial, thereby replacing the depth of interpersonal reflexive development with behavioral regimens for health. While these futures are being designed, extant social institutions lose the grounds for interactively formed personal identity, without yet having in place the new technosurface, healthy-lifestyle performer who complements

*This section is from a revised excerpt of a longer work. For a full study see Wexler, Philip (1992), *Becoming somebody: Toward a social psychology of school*. London: Falmer Press.

postmodernism's diffused spectator in consumption as a substitute for an identity or self. What we have described in our high-school studies are the struggles of youth in educational institutions during this transitional time.

What we found in the school case studies were conditioned patterns of social withdrawal that challenge the basic constituent elements of social relations, of "the social." Instead of grand theoretical challenges to the concept of society, or social relations, we described specific *institutional processes* that reverse establishment of society (Touraine, 1989). Instead of socialization, what we found was desocialization, or society in reverse.

These practical, institutional processes of social reversal represent a destruction of basic social elements, and, when taken together, indicate a reversal of society or, even an end of the social. Not a macro, epochal transformation of media against society, consumption rather than production, or informationalism replacing industry; but, a set of specific institutional social practices that are practical deconstructions of the social.

In each socioeconomic class we studied, typifying different social class segments, basic constituent aspects of social relations were being destroyed. In the working class, it was interaction. For the professional middle class, it was no longer, as Max Horkheimer and Theodor Adorno wrote (1972), that everyone was belabored by the social whole or totality. Rather, they were belabored by the absence of the social whole. Here it was society that was missing at the center of socioeconomic class social relations. For the urban, so-called underclass of mostly African American and Hispanic youths, virtually pre-school moral stigma and inferiorization made the self tenuous and, if not absent, then certainly under attack and acting to defend against an imminent absence. *Interaction, society and self* are basic elements of social relations that we found differentially expressed, in each school and socioeconomic class—but not by their realization or fullness. Instead, it is the emptying and lack of these practices and their representations that appears to stand at the center of what we may still call social life.

The emptying process is unintended and overdetermined in each case. The attenuation of dyadic interaction is a by-product of distrust created by the school administration, in harmony with its community, as it strives for order and respect. The direct effect, of course, is social selection, stratification and polarization of student peer groups. The resultant atmosphere is one of containment and suppression. On top of this pushing out of the ingredients of a full social center of interaction as an unintended by-product of the search for order and respect, there are additional sources or conditions that reinforce the process of emptying reciprocal, identifying, bonding, or socializing social interaction.

Teachers have taken one step from their overwhelmingly working-class origins, and they don't want to be reminded again, as professional adults now, how the bad manners and unclean appearance that students display can threaten to throw them back socially whence their parents had risen. Mass cultural difference reinforces class cultural difference and gives reason for a social distance opened up by fear, frustration, and a displacement of the teachers' own professional insecurity and threat from administrative surveillance, control, disrespect and uncertain employment. Family differences are part of the attribution of historically and culturally produced deficits among students. It is easier for teachers to forgive their own ritualistic self-distancing from the critical interaction induced by organizational and professional dynamics of failure and frustration if they can blame the students. It is easier to say of students than of oneself that "they don't deserve it."

The emptying of society is less perceptible, and can occur without projecting blame, in the professional middle-class school. Within the school as a teacher and as a student, one knows that personal self-definition and ambition is nestled within peer associations. Student stories of the pressures of parents and their peers' ambition show an articulated understanding of the social shaping of individual identities. Teachers may even acknowledge that their own professionalism causes a certain degree of social division by academic department. Students may complain about the "apathy" and lack of school spirit. Yet, these understandings appear as qualifications, addenda to the struggle for a self built only within a limited range of acceptable personal achievements, an ambitious self that ultimately pushes society out of the center of these intrasocial school and socioeconomic class relations only to complain about the corrosive effects of its absence.

In the urban school, students fight against the institutionalized process of emptying, because their selves are openly at stake. Emptying here is not of society, but of the self, and it occurs less behind the backs of the students than against their will. It is imposed forcibly, and out of fear, by their teachers and guards. The quest for control is not so much to restore respect for authorities. Rather, it is the sort of control of population management, an apparently logistical problem that presents itself as an issue of attendance. Teachers rationalize injuries to student selfhood as consequences of the need to manage students, individually and collectively—to rescue themselves from having to face the pedagogically onerous task of overcoming students' many earlier deprivations or their own fears of student violence. In-class quiet assignments avoid the pedagogical encounter, while so-called collectively regulated attacks mounted by deans and guards usually prevent any unmanageable forms of collective self-expression. They prevent problems of population management and aim to avoid the fear-inspiring uncontrollability of students when students are overly self-expressive outside the decaying forms of the old bureaucratic fortress of school. This vibrant student self is not harnessed and elevated, but pressed into corners and locked out by the steel doors of school time. Where the internal apparatus of control fails, the therapeutic and legal ministries reach beyond the school to the district and then to the city's welfare management system.

The process of self-formation or formation of identity as compensation for a social relational lack and as a defense against the absence of social structuring at the center of school life is not the whole story of how individual identities are socially produced. But, it is that part of the story that we saw enacted as high-school youths struggled to become somebody. What we saw is how much identity is created as a defensive compensation for a failure in modern social relations and how hints of a postmodern succession to modern social relations are already altering the terms of how society affects the self.

A more expansive view is that these school or socioeconomic class differences represent a divided self and identity work. When recomposed, this divided self offers a portrait of the fin-de-siecle self—or, more precisely, of an institutional prologue to a vaunted postmodern transformation of the self. Seen separately, these are self processes particular to each socioeconomic class segment: class psychology. Seen as a whole, there is an internally differentiated field upon which some historically new, postmodern or otherwise, sort of identity is created: historical psychology. Each school type and socioeconomic class segment represents an aspect of the self, just as each lack in either interaction, society, or self is an aspect of social relations.

The emptying of social relations induces a set of defensive self processes as compensation for the absence. In the working-class school a series of divisions or splits develops that protects against a vulnerability created by an absence of caring interaction and completed identification with adult authority. "Rads" and "jocks," "good kids" and "losers," and exaggerations of male and female, are some of the oppositions that occur within the absence of a consistent positive identification with a listening, though powerful, adult.

In its organizational separation between bureaucratic discipline and therapeutic understanding, the prototypical working-class high school that we studied mimics the stereotypical sex-role divisions of the patriarchal nuclear family. But, unlike the family, the organizational apparatus fails in the initial positive engagement with students. Teachers' own professional insecurities and career trajectories, community demands for a restoration of order and control, fiscal retrenchment, and a newer difference between students and their teachers, involving advancing mass culture and intensified economic need, all combine to dissipate the trust that might produce the caring identification necessary for reciprocal interaction. Division is the first line of defense, underlined and secured by exaggeration of differences. But the final victor is alienated identity formation in which not a self, but an image of self emerges. The mirror replaces the subject.

For the middle-class student, alienation or self-distancing is already part of the self. It is not the school structure that is seen as powerless and irrelevant from the start. Instead, through a combination of ironic humor and depression, the limitless performance expectations that are themselves integral to student identity, are put under control by dampening commitment to them.

Performance is at once the medium and goal of self-affirmation. But, it is also a threatening enemy of the self, because it can denigrate and reject the self when not properly pacified. The never-ending character of performance demands college that is beyond high school, and the career demands beyond college, and social conscience and economic status beyond career—and instigates strategies of dampening, depression and distance.

In students' terms "the idea of the school" represents a form of society that is hardly an antidote to an excessive emphasis on individual performance. "School spirit," like performance pressure, can unleash limitless expectations for commitment. Students can be committed to the United Nations club, math team or band. Those are delimited commitments that can be scheduled and contained in commitment of self as well as time. But, in the idea of the school, the concept of a larger society has become "nothing." On the surface, students are too busy achieving to have the energy to become part of something socially larger than themselves in what are commonly called "school activities." Beyond that, however, it is the character rather than the logistics of performance that diminishes collective capacities for society.

Socially created performance pressures carry along with them built-in defenses against limitlessness itself. These performance pressures represent means of self-affirmation, but also of unbounded threats to the self. They are channels of uncontrollable demand, unpredictability, and finally, of an unbounded self. The success ethic of our ideal, typical, professional middle-class school requires ability to engage limitlessness, but in a controlled way. "Mellowing out" or getting "psyched down" is a means of self-defense against performance.

Apathy is the students' way of describing the compensatory defense against limitless demand that is represented by both performance and society. Performance can be individualized and regulated by depression. The denial and negation of society is part of a compensatory defense against limitless demand and the threat of an unbounded self that is represented by performance. It is, practically, more difficult to withdraw from school performance pressures. Society, however, can be denied. It can be evaporated into nothing. It can become a haunting absence for which apathy is simply a condensed label. Depression is a method of self-defense and rationalized communication is a way out of social fragmentation and an absent social center. Social apathy, even though society seems missed, still operates to keep performance "on track."

Social institutions, even by their lacks, shape the self. There is, however, a difference between the interactional and society lack in working-class and professional middle-class schools and a more basic lack of self-affirmation in the urban, poor, minority or so-called underclass school. Self-establishment has to be repeatedly accomplished before any other direction or shaping takes place. The compensatory process is more direct. Where the lack of self-affirmation is the basic social absence, the socially patterned defensive self-formation occurs at the first, basic line of self-defense: self-existence.

From the first hellos to the last good-byes, the students work to create a visible, differentiated and reputable self. The moral language of being "good" or "decent" is the way in which the social comes to be represented in demarginalizing self-existence. Whatever they may have to prove about their self-value at the outset of their school career is exaggerated by the school's organization around the assumption that what is lacking in the students is a decent, moral self. Morality here is not the neat, clean concern of the upwardly mobile working-class teacher, but again, a more basic issue that places in question the strength of student integrity. From the first early-morning meetings of the administrative staff to the close of the school day, the students are managed, at worst as a potentially dangerous population, and at best, as a deficit self, to be classified, guided or uplifted.

"Drillin'" is the name of a social interaction game of verbal, invidious self-distinction and fighting that almost always works as self-defense against imputed moral inferiority. The absence of an affirmed, valuable self induces expressive displays of self-marking as the most immediate and accessible compensation for schools' reinforcement of socially inherited stigma.

Taken together, these defensive processes of a self formed within institutions characterized by social practices of emptying core elements of social relations are more revealing of what postmodern society means practically than any general, textualist talk about a "decentered," postmodern self. While our description only tells part of the story, it ties self dynamics to organized social practices in concrete, everyday institutional life. What I have presented is a class-divided self, formed as a compensatory defense against a class-specific institutional lack in social relations. It shows, contrary to the usual postmodern view, an unwillingness to accept centrifugal self-dissipation as an easy herald of a new ahistorical epoch. Identity is formed as a defense against social absences, not in welcoming acceptance of them.

A potentially emergent postmodern self would emerge out of social interactional labor for preserving the self against social lacks and beyond the first line of more directly compensatory actions of self-construction. These actions, despite evident overlap, are class-specific strategies of self-defense and self-construction. They offer a guide to differences in process and formative practices of the class-self. The class-specific typical selves are, respectively, divided, distant and displayed.

Alternatives

It is possible that elite, corporatist, integrated-control and institutional social evacuation can continue without any further cultural response, and indeed, without even culture. But, if it has done nothing else, postmodernism has shown that culture has not vanished. Yet, the character of culture postmodernism describes does not offer the cultural basis for an alternative. Rather, it extends the overintegrated, socially emptying society to culture, and so destroys the opportunity for culturally constituting an alternative.

Carlo Mongardini describes this extension by saying that: "Postmodernism becomes the last ideology adopted by modernity to save itself. . . . Like it or not, postmodernism marks the end of the old order" (Mongardini, 1990:56, 58) Postmodernism aestheticizes modernity's unqualified embrace of change that is an engine of the instrumental economic approach and values that Marxism did not eliminate. The effect is to continue modernity's economistic and rationalistic reduction of culture to privatism, fragmentation and neo-romantic exaltation of momentary experience. Ultimately what is lost is not only the individual but also the "moral passions, religion, solidarity . . . and spiritual culture, life-giving tendencies, and symbolic structures" to an excessively abstract, instrumental rationalism. Postmodernism becomes "the last ideology of modernism" that maintains modernism's values, but does so incoherently and generates a "crisis of identity which passes from the level of the individual to the entire culture" (Mongardini, 1990: 55, 59, 61).

Even those who see postmodern culture as the sign of a phoenix rising from the ashes (Olalquiaga, 1992) recognize it as the cultural expression of modern society that continues a range of social processes: "taking commodity fetishism to the extreme;" glorifying consumption and engaging in compulsively repetitive imaging work and the "fragmentation, intertextuality, and massive commodification of everyday life that began with modernity." The "transfer of time to space", the loss of historicity that both Olalquiaga and Harvey portray as characteristically postmodern, is part of the same cultural incoherence and symbolic disruption asserted by Mongardini, with the same result:

> This disruption of the symbolic unity radically transforms experience, since it no longer is connected to a transcendent, abstract meaning. Instead, experience becomes intense and ma-

> terial, seeking the confirmation of its existence in the present and concrete. (Olalquiaga,1992:22)

Stjepan Mestrovic describes the experiential aspect in more conventional sociological terms, calling postmodernism "the institutionalization of anomie," which "can be likened to an addiction," where the " postmodern self is bored, and demands an increase in the quantity of stimulation" (1991:204,207). Carlos Castoriadis describes postmodernism as a "generalized conformism":

> Agreeably mixing up with the fashionable loose talk about "pluralism" and "respect for the difference of the other," it ends up with a glorification of eclecticism, a covering up of sterility and the generalization of the "anything goes" principle. . . . (1992:22)

Similarly, Axel Honneth describes an "artificial pluralization of aesthetically shaped lifeworlds" that "empty subjectivity motivationally so that the electronic media can then compensatively encroach on this emptied subjectivity with its offers of simulation" (1992: 26, 27).

Postmodern culture does not provide conditions to counter the integrated rationalization of control or resources for social relations to realize identity in other than hypermedia, baroque compensations. There appears to be no point of reliable resistance, against which there is an opening to create "the foundations of a new culture" (Mongardini, 1990).

Both the patriarchal presence of authority (Benjamin, 1988) and the postmodern so-called absence of authority prevent any dialectic of differentiation and so reinforce social control and integration as well as cultural and identity eclecticism and conformity. The reinvention of a dialectic of differentiation depends on *real difference*, as Jean-Marie Vincent (1991) puts it, on "the rediscovery of the sacred amidst profane activities prevailing in everyday life." The primary resistance to a rationalizing, commodifying "colonization of the lifeworld" is not attained only in language, but is also present in a socioemotional, interactional, existential process that severs the authority transferences and countertransferences that structure everyday institutional life.

Difference is not mere differentiation, even from a distant point, as a structuralist reading would have it. Difference is created, ultimately, in light of an historic experience or memory of creation. As Hans Jonas (1974:37) writes:

> To be called forth from nothing and to exist only by constant renewal of this act, assures each individual of the immediate interest of the creative cause and so makes it interesting in itself.

Becoming ensnared both in authority and in its absence is a displacement of desire. It is a distorted substitution for the desire for transformation through which sacred otherness sheds a transformative temporal light on what is normally thought to be mundane. Scenarios of self-formation and struggle against ambiguous, diminished, depersonalized and therapeutically disarmed forms of authority can be replaced by what they have themselves replaced: sacred otherness that occupies time "inassimilable by automatic mechanisms." (Vincent, 1991)

In this view, the cultural resources required for a dereifying moment may be found in a cultural creation that is based in absolute, rather than naturalistic, differences and enables interaction, dialogue and receptivity to "otherness" in the widest sense.

This view of culture is neither a melancholic embrace of novel experience in the megalopolis, nor the performance anticulture of American liberalism, nor simply the moral conservatives' reassertion of so-called traditional values. These are the currently available cultural responses to a new social regime that we see emerging in the core self-formative educational institutions. Harvey first describes how "the emphasis upon ephemerality, collage, fragmentation, and dispersal in philosophical and social thought mimics the conditions of flexible accumulation." He then goes on to say: "But it is exactly at this point that we encounter the opposite reaction that can best be summed up as the search for personal and collective identity, the search for secure moorings in a shifting world" (1989:302).

The collective identity solution to the modern/postmodern destruction of culture and identity consists not only of a reaction, not only of the moral majority's early attack on secular humanism in education or its recent electoral politics of "family values." It also includes the radical "new" movements, which are Carlo Mongardini's, Alberto Melucci's (1989), and others' hopes for a culturally rooted alternative to integrated control, social emptying and conformism. Even the new radical social movements are subject to a continuing process of societal incorporation (to say nothing here of the failure of the "old" radicalism, in theory and in practice, despite its academic popularity.) Do they exemplify that "genuine critical spirit" Cornelius Castoriadis calls for against postmodern conformism, a critical spirit which "can only exist in and through the establishment of a distance with what there is, entailing the conquest of a point of view beyond the given, therefore in the work of creation" (1992:22). Postmodern conformist culture results from a more profound problem of the "decadence of spiritual creation."

Postmodern idolatry substitutes practical consumptionist commentary on commodities for earlier authorities. Radical theory reinforces rather than breaks the hold of the mundane, because it is not truly different, despite its command of a plurality of languages of difference, critique and even transcendence ("Suddenly, holiness is all over the place," Olalquiaga, 1992:37).

Creation, from the point of view of sacred otherness—which is neither Durkheim's and Basil Bernstein's static "differentiation," (a recontextualized serialization of the rituals of "havdala," or differentiation, as I shall argue) nor Adorno and Horkehiemer's "transcendental subject of cognition"—is an existential, utopia-driven, practical desire for recognition, dialogue, openness and receptivity to both an unreified state and the living other that extends to primordial moments of creation and encounter. In Judaism, following Abraham Heschel and Franz Rosenzweig and even Eric Fromm, I would call it the "eternal Sabbath." It is the truly different, opposite to contemporary forms of idolatry, and it is the starting point for articulating educational alternatives to the Toyota school.

This sort of fundamental cultural creation is an existential and practical "calling" and not a bibliographical display or critique of postmodern exegesis. In education, it will mean teaching toward utopia, not toward performance-driven techniques and external standards. "What matters," Martin Buber wrote, "is that time and again an older generation, staking its entire existence on that act, comes to a younger with the desire to teach, waken, and shape it; then the holy spark leaps across the gap" (1963:139).

The End of Puritan Sociology

The sociocultural changes that contain the dynamic polarities of intensified secularization in rationalistic commodification and a sacralization that yearns for excess and simplicity might be represented in sociology. Yet ordinarily in sociology, recognition of the immersion of the changing conceptual content of the discipline in wider currents of sociocultural change is generally ignored or denied.

Even now—after the critique of ideology has been institutionally tamed and represented as postmodern diversity by sinecured humanists self-righteously promoting legitimation—American academics remain notably unreflexive about the meaning of their work in relation to larger historical and cultural contexts. Sociology's fashion changes are at best seen as an adaptation to intellectual trends. So, now postmodernism has to be considered, at least by the theorists, as an intellectual fashion with implications for sociology (Seidman, 1991; Arditi, 1993). But, the sociological method of intellectual appropriation is idealist; postmodernism, or any other trend, becomes important as an idea, and not as a representation or aspect of a changing form of social life or larger set of historical and culturally lived circumstances.

The wished-for sociological best-case scenario is that the current Democratic administration in the United States may reinvigorate safe, apparatus-management sociology and its liberal ideology that has been renovated by postmodern rationales for pluralism. Sociologists will be better able to practice what John O'Neill calls "sociological nemesis," feeding off

> the normalization and abnormalization processes in the individual and social body [which are] two sides of a single practice which continuously expands the social sciences as administrative disciplines in the therapeutic society. (1986:26)

There was, however, a reflexive moment in American sociology, during the late sixties and early seventies, when the field was not simply understood as a clumsy marriage of idea and technique, but instead was analyzed socially and culturally as an historical cultural practice of concrete, identifiable social strata. The main theme in the radical reflexive analysis was that, as Dusky Lee Smith put it, "in varying degrees, the founding fathers of American sociology were ideological protagonists for corporate capitalism" (1970:68). The reconsideration of sociology as an ideology of social control was then part of a more general reassessment of American social reform movements, especially Progressivism, and their role in the establishment and propagation of the "corporate liberal state" (Weinstein, 1968; Slaughter, 1975; Schwendinger and Schwendinger, 1974). Sociology was "the academic counterpart" (Shaskolsky, 1970:12) of liberal social reform.

In 1970, Alvin Gouldner published *The Coming Crisis of Western Sociology*, which emphasized less the liberal Progressivist and corporatist origins and affinities of American sociology and more its various linkages to a broader culture of utilitarianism. The so-called crisis of sociology was brought forward by a new generation of modern radicals of the New Left. Their critique of sociology was not simply of the scientific failures of functionalism, but also of the conservative social effects of academic sociology. Both in his explanation of this challenge to sociology and in his prognosis, Gouldner countered the customary idealist abstraction of sociology from culture:

> My reading of the contemporary radical condition is that we are now living in a fluid transitional era when a younger generation has emerged with a sharply different structure of sentiments, with collective feelings that are not resonated by the very different kinds of sentiments that have been historically deposited in older theories, and this makes some among the younger generation either coldly indifferent or hotly antagonistic to the older theories. There is, in short, a gap between the newly emerging structure of sentiments among young radicals and the older languages or theories, a gap that has not yet been bridged by the development of a new theoretical language in which the young radicals might more fully express themselves and their own conception of reality. (1970:7)

In part, Gouldner understood the "new radicals'" revolt against various sociological expressions of utilitarian culture as a crisis of meaning: "Much of the new radicalism today is a response to the meaninglessness of success rather than to the lack of it" (1970:407). He wrote that:

> In the end, I suspect the future sociology of the New Left will seek both an economically sensitive neo-Marxism, which has an 'opening' toward the practicality of utilitarianism, and a morally sensitive or critical sociology, *open to a critique of the system from some external standpoint* [emphasis added]. (1970:409)

Gouldner's understanding of the basis of sociology's crisis and the possible resolution of this crisis is amplified, I think, by replacing sociology not simply in utilitarian culture (and in reactions against it), but in more foundational discourses—particularly within American religion. C. Wright Mills, in an early paper on the sociology of sociology (1943), offered a content analysis of social problems texts to argue that they represented a "professional ideology of social pathologists" whose world view was deeply reflective of small-town American Protestantism. In the reflexive sixties and seventies work that Mills greatly influenced, even the corporate liberal critics acknowledged the religious context of sociology.

> The conservative nature of sociology may perhaps be traced to the political climate of this region which became the bedrock of both moderate conservative political thinking and of moderate reform philosophy. This dualism in turn seems to stem from the personal life-histories of many of the leading figures of this period. As the Hinkles have pointed out, most of the early presidents of the American Sociological Association came from rural backgrounds and "grew to maturity at a time when the religious and ethical tradition of Protestantism still dominated the nation. Often their reformism was a secular version of the Christian concern with salvation and redemption and was a direct outgrowth of religious antecedents in their personal lives." (Hinkle and Hinkle, 1954; discussed by Shakolsky, 1970:15)

The replacement of sociology in culture, and particularly the view of American sociology as shaped within Protestantism, is extensively argued in the more recent work of Vidich and Lyman (1985, 1986). They see in the pervasive methodological positivism and persistent interest in understanding and creating a national community a strong recontextualization of religious belief into American social theory: "Virtually all American sociologists converted issues of theodicy into problems for sociodicy" (1985:281). And, "from the beginning, sociological thought in the United States had its roots in the Protestant religion" (1986:44). Vidich and Lyman explained that early American sociologists of the mid-nineteenth century welcomed Comtean positivism, which had "ideological affinities" with Protestantism:

> The positivism of American sociology owes much of its outlook to Puritan practicality and to the Puritan impulse to engineer the perfection of American society and the world. Fundamentally it reflected the idea that rational Christians could find rational solutions to social and political problems. This notion helped merge America's special variant of the Protestant ethic with

> technocentric positivism and the optimistic spirit inherited from the French Enlightenment. (1985:4)

The description of "transvaluation from theodicy to sociodicy" centers on the ways in which sociology became a secularized expression of the American Protestant quest for a "holy commonwealth". The desired national community, and efforts to understand and actualize its shared moral basis are traced to both the Puritan ideal of a "redeemer nation" and the cultural work of restoring the lost authority of Puritanism to the nation, in a more secularized form. Vidich and Lyman (1986) argue that American pragmatism was the mediating language between the lost Puritan community and the secularized moral/national question of founding American sociologists. George Herbert Mead, for example, is interpreted as secularizing his pragmatic predecessor Josiah Royce's Christian community as "the generalized other":

> Mead's social psychology has retained a conception of the moral individual in a secular world. His conception of the generalized other as each individual's moral arbiter in the secular world allowed him to reformulate the religious ethics of a Puritan community into the civil moralities of a secular society. (1986:48)

This same idea—that sociological theory can be understood as a secularization of Protestantism—has been argued for the more complex history of European sociology as well. Geoffrey Hawthorn's *Enlightenment and Despair* finds commonality across differences of national sociologies and individual orientations in "the Protestantism that they shared, the assumption of the spiritual, moral and cognitive autonomy of the individual" (1976:112). But more than it stresses either individualism or a quest for moral community, classical sociology—even as reaction against Enlightenment philosophy—espouses commitment to what Hawthorn aptly terms "the monistic moral confidence of the rationalists."

Of course, the broader view within which this discussion of the Puritan Protestantism of sociology is embedded is Weber's concept of general secularization: the historical, social psychological transformation of Puritanism to an innerworldly, ascetic, rationalizing economic ethic. My interest here is not to defend or extend Weber's thesis to the origins of sociology itself, case by case. Rather, the point is to recontextualize sociology in social life and cultural history as an element in a larger reflexive project that aims to relate the future of sociology to those wider sociocultural changes. The Puritan Protestant and, in a most general sense, the related Enlightenment, origins of sociology, become important now because that deeper cultural context of a secularized, transvalued set of connections between Protestantism and the culture we have come to call simply "modernity" is challenged, if not eroded, by cultural movements that the academy pulls together under the label "postmodernism."

The relevance of postmodernism to sociology is not as an ideational resource for fashionable borrowings, or even as a means to question its philosophical premises of foundationalism, essentialism, "rational monism," individualism, and so on. The interest rather is that postmodernism might signal a new culture, a new form of life and challenge to the deeper religious and cultural bases of sociological thought and practice. Postmodernism is relevant to our speculation about the future of sociology because it is a sign of the erosion of the "modern," Puritan cultural foundations of the discourse of the discipline. Advocates for postmodernism want to announce the end of Enlightenment modernity, and I add, Protestant, culture. If sociology is what Hawthorn terms a "secular cosmology," then it too recedes with modernity, and its future must be sought in an interpretive, even speculative reading of alternative life patterns and cultural ethics—in an emergent cultural foundation.

If it is true that the culture of the current age is not merely fragmented, and is expressed not as centered and "social," but as *apparently* desocialized individualized practices, then incipient or virtual collective cultural forms are emergent and need to be extrapolated from individual practices. This makes speculation about the future of sociology even more difficult: first, we must locate a future sociology within its cultural context; and second, we must identify that context from its dispersed and individualized shards of practice and meaning. By exploring those practices and emergent cultural forms, we may be better able to describe what to expect after Puritan sociology has had its day.

Between Commodity and Sacred

What postmodernism does take further and transforms in quality is the modern contradiction between emancipation and control, or, in Weber's terms, between charismatic and rational. The medium or channel through which the contradiction operates is itself contradictory and further polarized under the postmodern regime. For as modern individualism intensifies, so does the hypersocialized, disciplinary society. The pursuit of lonely, individualistic self-freedom coexists with "colonization of the life world" (Habermas, 1987) and therapeutically coded extensions of the administered society that is Enlightenment's ironic (Horkheimer and Adorno, 1972) and unhappy ending.

The extreme point of rationalization—which, like sociology, has its cultural roots in Protestantism (Weber, 1958)—is the pervasiveness of the commodity form, the commodification of all aspects of everyday life. The extreme point of the counter tendency, "charisma" in Weber's terminology, is expressed in what Wuthnow (1992) calls the "rediscovery of the sacred." Between an overarching dynamic structural contradiction of processes of commodification on the one hand and processes of resacralization on the other (Thompson, 1990) are found a range of individual practices of adaptation and transformation that simultaneously reflect and presage their "intellectual sublimations" as cultural forms. Sociology—or, to use a term less institutionally bound to current academies, social analysis—of the future is the socially reflexive aspect of these cultural forms.

What occurs between polarities of commodification and sacralization? I argue that the self is the central site of structural contradiction and that culture-creating movements increasingly are embedded in collective processes of self-transformation. (For an expanded discussion, see Wexler, 1991).

The primary social basis of a movement that works through the process of self-transformation is the contradiction between the subjective demands of consumption and production. The initial youth movement of the professional middle class, like historical movements generally (Alberoni, 1984; Foss and Larkin, 1986), required the sense of a new and other world, which included a radical reorganization of the self or ego. A new movement is possible that is created from contradictory socially structured, subjectively experienced demands experienced as *ambivalence.*

Social contradictions are the precondition for the sort of ego ambivalence that Alberoni (1984: 84-125) describes as the core of the "nascent state":

> one, eros, violently seizing new objects in its grasp, and the other destroying the structures that imprison the former and investing the old love objects. Compared to the obsessive constraint that preceded it, the experience is one of liberation.(1984:102)

Ambivalence or internal conflict can, however, be contained by patterned methods of ego defense, as we saw in studies of the school/class self. Cultural mediation of the self/society relation now performs that function. The analyses of David Ashley, Laurie Langman, Timothy Luke and others (Wexler, 1991; Schneider, 1975; Slater, 1980) describe postmodern forms of commodity fetishism. How the socially patterned defenses that contain ambivalence work from the mass culture to the organizational level (Hirschhorn, 1988; LaBier, 1989) still requires a good deal more description. The collective/self relation is mediated by culturally reinforced and culturally represented obsession and compulsion as well as fetishism and addiction. The study of collective neurosis that postmodernism and its critics describe corresponds to typical self dynamics in the consumption relation. The "spectacular self" is television's self (Kroker and Cook, 1986). Self-limitation and neurosis is, however, also created for the "working wounded" (LaBier, 1989) in the postindustrial workplace (Hirschhorn, 1988). Postmodernism sublimates necessity and performance as well as sexual desire; its representation, even critically, is of the culture of consumption.

Still the career is no less powerful a determinant of the life-world among the professional middle class than is its free-time commodified fetishism of visual imagination. While the self is spectacular or even imploded, it is simultaneously over-instrumentalized. If self-reflection is eliminated by absorption into pervasive media image and sound, practical action is rationalized into increasingly informationalized structures of decision making. What Noble (1991) describes in the genesis of the "man-machine symbiosis" paradigm in military/educational research is the end point of a more self-invested and self-mediated organization of worklife. The consumer self is diffused while the producer self is condensed. One is attached to its object fetishistically, while the other is tied by disembodied performance obsession.

This contradiction is socially structured between production and consumption and subjectively experienced between the happily dissolute and the seriously retentive self (Langman, 1991). The intense press toward self-organization will occur when the now protected boundaries of the institutionally split self give way to integrative forces. The press for integration is economic rationalization for a more efficient subjectivity. Ultimately, the quest for greater performance and productivity, under the intermediate guise of "healthfulness," demands an end to defensive ego-wastefulness. There is a way out of the iron cage: rationalization destroys the internal defenses that help reproduce it. The new movement is a deformed, revised holism, one that will have to redevelop self and social integration from the residues of the historic contradiction of an agonized leading class, and as we shall see, this holism cannot avoid a sacred hue.

The localization of social energies at the site of the self of course prompts the direction of commodifying and not only "transformative" possibilities, to self dynamics. For "the agonized leading class," the professional middle class, self-activity can be quickly territorialized as "life-style engineering":

> Functional rationality now becomes sinister indeed. It permeates the private lives of people just as it dominates the public sphere. It undermines all traditions. It makes even more precarious the individual's quest for meaning and identity.
>
> The new professions apply an engineering mindset to the searing questions arising from the modern crisis of meaning and identity, a crisis to which modern production with its manifold tensions has significantly contributed. (Kellner and Heuberger, 1992:13)

These are the new professions of cultural workers, who, with a strongly individualistic and moral outlook help to create a "liberation market" of services for personalized self-realization, by "creating" and distributing "designer life-styles." Significantly, James Davison Hunter and Tracy Fessenden (1992) write that life-style engineering and self-realization is not the merely hedonistic activity that might be imagined. On the contrary, the search for self is very much a moral need, which is the condition for a new brand of postindustrial, capitalist "moral entrepreneurs" who "derive their livelihood from the production and distribution of new ways of thinking and acting morally" (1992:161). Their moralities are generally secular, even body-centered, with special emphasis on the moralization of health (they are anti-smoking, pro-animal rights). For Hunter and Fessenden, these new moral entrepreneurs work to produce an as yet inchoate new moral order, by and for the new class:

> then it is to the knowledge sector, and to the categories of people we have called moral entrepreneurs in particular, that we must look to see how a newer moral order—one that greases the wheels of postmodern capitalism—takes shape. (1992:187)

Existing simultaneously with the investment of social energies in the self-production of healthful remoralized sectors of the new professional middle class within commodified postmodern capitalism, the self and its dynamics—what I call "individual practices"—are contemporary versions of charisma that are expressed in antirational, individualized processes of self-loss, fusion or transcendence. Following Sigmund Freud, Charles Lindholm explains charisma as a reaction and countertendency to excessive "civilization":

> the rationalization of society may actually exaggerate the human yearning for self-loss in the passionate mob gathered around the charismatic. This is because the ever greater restrictions of civilized life and bureaucratic organization of necessity increasingly frustrate instinctual demands—in particular the demand for ecstatic experiences of merger. Heightened repression means that charisma, which satisfies the desire for self-loss, will be revealed in an excessive and convulsive manner . . . according to Freudian theory. (1990:60-61)

Lindholm attempts to specify the Freudian need for self-loss as a social response, not simply to instinctual repression but to modern conditions of alienation and then to postmodern conditions of loss of self boundaries within an ideology of possessive individualism. Postmodernism's "play ethic" is "more a precondition than a defense against charismatic involvement"(1990:87) since it contributes to emotional distancing and loss of self boundary markers (For description of the postmodern self, see also Gergen, 1991).

The need for ecstatic self-loss or deep spiritual attachment and merger or fusion becomes a counterweight to a postmodern condition. It is one that continues and heightens modernity's commitments at once to self, rationalization, and the dissolution of tradition and at the same time to the lack of self boundaries, narcissism and emotional detachment of postmodernity.

Lindholm explores different paths, as varied as religious movements and romantic love, to underline how the "primal need" for passionate attachment and ecstatic loss in a charismatic object is variously, but widely, expressed. This quest for "a communion that offers not reason, but lived vitality," this "electrifying blurring of boundaries," will continue to exist. "The question," he concludes, "is what form these moments will take" (1991:189).

A similar effort to discover paths out of "the iron cage," although more in the Marxist language of alternatives to commodification, is expressed in the work of Vincent (1991). For her,

> the real need is to grasp the emerging movements against the tyranny of abstract labour, in social relations as well as in intersubjectivity, in individuals' relation to their vital environment as well as to their action. (1991:141)

It is not labor, but art, for all its "many dead-ends," that offers an "anticipatory force," a "going beyond immediate relations" of capitalist valorization and abstraction to a politics "that is no longer, in its essence, the strategy or tactics of conquering positions of power; it becomes a struggle for better conditions of action, for fuller communication allowing for a greater social inventiveness" (1991:140). Art is "subversion" and "nourishment," a secular sacred "inassimilable" moment against the persuasiveness of a commodified everyday life.

This dynamic—the contradiction between emancipatory and controlling practices under postmodern conditions—is described also by Alberto Melucci (1989) in his theory of social movements. The dialectic, of course, is that the same "hypersocialized" controlling system also creates needs and capacities that counter its reproduction. In a vein similar to Harvey's (1989) postmodern flexible accumulation capitalism, Melucci explains how "complex societies" dissolve time, space, and identity boundaries. Although control and pathologies intensify, so also does individual awareness and a sense of life possibilities and choice. Individuation proceeds along with both the disappearance of "grand narratives" and the prevalence of technologies of social control, creating along the way greater pressure for a meaningful life.

The location of social contradiction on the self site, identity, is further localized in a dialectic of the body. At once medicalized in the therapeutic society, a "new body culture" "reveals a human dimension which is neither reducible to instrumental rationality nor stamped with the sign of darkness or perversion." (Melucci, 1989:123)

The dynamic is that: "Faced with this expanding control, it is as if the body is mobilizing the resources of 'nature' to safeguard a non-manipulated identity." There is an "ambiguity" of the body between liberatory self-consciousness and manipulated medicalization in which the body is "a resource of social control"; "bodily satisfaction is an effective guarantee of social control" (1989:124). Individualism itself becomes the medium of a "postmaterial society" where the liberatory, transforming potential resides in a belief in the individual's right to a more meaningful existence, which serves as the social psychological basis of claims for freedom and democracy. The body crystallizes the contradiction and its possibilities, in a parallel to charismatic ecstasy and fusion, or to a politically subversive art.

Resacralization and its Social Analytic

Jurgen Habermas (1987) also describes this dynamic—an alternative culture arising from individual practices and leading to a new society—and leaves open for speculation the forms that potential alternatives to an administered, "colonized" lifeworld might take. Alternatives may be "painful manifestations of deprivation in a culturally impoverished and one-sidedly rationalized practice of everyday life" (1987:395). Here too the dialectic is that the "system," which places the "symbolic structures of the lifeworld as a whole in question, can account for why they have become accessible to us." Following Habermas, Robert Wuthnow sees emergent religious movements as "protests against the growing bureaucratization and monetarization of the life world" (1992:141). In an analysis that focuses on American religion, Wuthnow underlines that the new American religious movements consciously manipulate symbols and center especially on "questions of personal meaning and purpose" (1992:99). Religion is not disappearing, but adapting to a changing societal context. The continued, if not intensified, interest in religion supports Thompson's argument that: "The various social processes that have been held to characterize modernization and modernity can themselves generate countervailing tendencies—secularization provokes sacralizing reactions" (1990:164). In Thompson's terminology, there are "striking revivals of cults of sacred community in the modern world" (Thompson, 1990:172).

Resacralization is also subject to incorporation, rationalization and commodification. Reducing the charisma of the body and soul to a mundane level can be seen in the example of the American mass movement for "recovery" (Kaminer, 1992). In what can only be described as "revival" movements, across America, both in small groups and in mass media, a disease of codependence has been discovered. All forms of compulsive behavior are described as addictions resulting from dependence on someone else's behavior, particularly that of family members. Modeled on Alcoholics Anonymous, there is a standard liturgy, a "twelve-step method" (a methodology of salvation, in Weber's sociology of religion) that can lead the "recovering" alcoholic, overeater, shopper, anythinger, to a "rebirth" of discovering the "inner child." Combining religious redemption with a secularized salvation methodology of peer-guided recovery, the twelve-step method is a secular cosmology that is transparently both sacred and commodified, operating at the self site to offer bodily-centered redemption by lowering the meaning of individual identity and social relation to the level of the routine.

For Wendy Kaminer it is "an ideology of salvation by grace" (1992:3). More than they resemble group therapy, twelve-step groups are like revival meetings, carrying on the pietistic tradition. From our point of view, the twelve-step method successfully merges secular and sacred, bodily and spiritual, and individual and collective needs. It is an effective social technology for postmodern salvation by reconstruction of meaningful and communicable mass, individually "recovered" identities. The twelve steps begin with an acknowledgment of powerlessness, go on to include statements of religious faith, and conclude with evangelical commitment to help move others from "denial to recovery" (1992:71).

Like the postmodern dialectic of the body, twelve-step methods are only part of a wider contemporary movement of "rediscovery of the sacred"; or, resacralization. The question is whether and how such individuated, if not quite "customized," dialectics become the bases of new cultures, which, from our point of view, would include social reflexivity, or a secular cosmology of a new social analytic. The key to such a cultural emergence is the articulation and elaboration of these individuated practices into a more general theory, or theodicy. Weber criticized his contemporaries precisely for remaining at the level of individual experience, without articulating the implied structure of beliefs:

> A religious revival [we might read, instead, "cultural renewal"] has never sprung from such a source. In the past, it was the work of intellectuals to sublimate the possession of sacred values into a belief in "redemption." (1946:280)

While sociological intellectuals have mostly remained aloof from such efforts, the literary critic Harold Bloom charts a course from literary criticism, which has been a model for postmodern sociologists, to what he calls "religious criticism." What Bloom portrays in his religious criticism is an American revivalism, undergirded not by Puritanism, but by a more primal, self-centered emphasis on knowing. Gnosticism, not Puritanism, is the basis of an American religion that comes to define cultural and public life. Bloom writes:

> And the American Religion, for its two centuries of existence, seems to me irretrievably Gnostic. It is knowing, by and of an uncreated self, or self-within-the-self, and the knowledge leads to freedom, a dangerous and doom-eager freedom: from nature, time, history, community and other selves. (1992:49)

More directly, he observes: "Awareness, centered on the self, is faith for the American Religion" (1992:54). Early in his essay, he characterizes the underlying themes of what he calls the American Religion:

> core of the American Religion: orphic, gnostic, millenarian. Other religions have promised us Eternity; only the American religion promises what Freud tells us we cannot have: "an improved infancy," as Hart Crane called it. (1992:31)

In both commodified (twelve-step method) and sacred (American Religion) forms of culture, individual-centered practices are generalized, often unifying both tendencies. Sociology can become a reflection of, and reflect on, these simultaneously individuated and collective processes. If Bloom is right in his dissection of the American self-religion, and if Habermas, Melucci, Lindholm, Harvey, and others are right about the centrality of self dynamics in postmodern, flexible-accumulation, hypersocialized, administered, colonized capitalism, emphasis increasingly will focus on the self—in both body and soul. The body, as both refuge from and instrument of the extant social regime, will be theorized not only in relation to culture, but, more scientifically, as a biological, psychosocial process. The "soul" will reenter public language as popular cultural and political rhetoric become openly religiously discursive.

Bloom's "religious criticism" is, I think, a response to this discursive shift, and I expect that we can see sociologies that not only ask religious questions, but are grounded in theodicies, more or less openly and self-consciously. The analytic secularization of these theodicies should be sought more in Gnostic than Puritan traditions, and more in contemplative emissary prophecies, in innerworldly "ecstaticism," and not more in asceticism. That means more attention to mysticism and to dissenting and esoteric tendencies within all of the major religions. The self-centered, anti-institutional "roads to salvation" (Weber, 1958) will increasingly become the cultural "soul" basis for both sacred and secular cosmologies of social understanding.

Bloom's *American Religion* rightly reminds us of the epic, national poem *Song of Myself,* by the American ecstatic archetypical anti-father, Walt Whitman, the poet of "the body and the soul," which proclaims:

> I celebrate myself, and sing myself
> And what I assume you shall assume,
> For every atom belonging to me as good belongs to you.

A future sociology that departs the liberal apparatus will become a sociology of the body and of the soul. Its language will be transparently religious, mystical, Gnostic and self-centered in orientation. It will also be physicalist, biochemical, and holistic, in the effort to connect individuated practices to intersubjectivity as social action and to social relations and aggregates as a science of the bio-psycho-social. Information on these channels will be both sacred and commodified, and Weber's analysis of methods to avoid and explain suffering and to achieve and rationalize ecstasy—a social psychology of religious action—will be replayed in new and different ways.

At its heart will be the quest for redemption from the new order, which will be conflictually inscribed in the everyday politics of struggles for integration, self-loss, and transcendence—of the body and the soul, and, above all, of their integration. We will come from a critique of alienation, through a deconstructive, postmodern sociology of absence, to an integrative, creative sociology of presence.

Sociology of Education

How we have arrived at a sociology of presence, in the sociology of education, for example, requires at least a quick look backward to articulate the changing premises or basic assumptions of the field. Retrospection goes against the grain of aggressive anticipation and the comfort of forward-looking, progressive imaginations. At the same time, it is fraught with pitfalls of nostalgia's false security and the self-serving interest of narcissism, encoded in legitimating, political terms. Its value is in remembrance of origins, articulation of continuity, and possibilities offered for integration. These values are antithetical to the ethos of postmodernism, with its antitemporal stance and its hostile bemusement with the expression of integrative aspirations within a dispersed field or space. But, I believe that these values become meaningful with the emergence of new social cosmologies in a new age.

Even more against the present mood of complacent pluralism and ironically resigned fetishism in postmodern commodities, the continuity I find even in a very brief sociology of education retrospection is in the quest for meaning and the desire for dealienated being. The drive, in at least my own work, has been consistently to place theory and research in this specialized field within a broader historical and cultural context. And, this contextualizing itself has been part of an effort to make academic work part of the same subjective, experiential desire for dealienation, for a better, more fully realized life, a desire that we frequently forget was as central a motive for the cultural revolution as any structural "political" goal.

Each phase of the recent history of the field has been at least parallel, if not integral, to broader cultural changes. Like the wider cultural movements, "the field," or its "carriers," moved forward by challenging current assumptions, cultural as well as scientific, only to see the routinization and decadence of its challenge, followed by a new, "charismatic" challenge to the culture. The character of the challenge, its channel or modality, has changed twice before, and I think that it is now changing again. Also, the depth or extent of the cultural and scientific challenge has increased in each successive phase. Speaking broadly, I see a succession of political, aesthetic, and religious dominant cultural modalities, within which the sociology of education enacted this scenario of challenge and decadence.

I described the origins of the political phase, in the American context, as a challenge to the culture of Progressivism, and to its academic representation in the liberal positivist sociology of education as incited by the then Black movement and the Student movement. In the aesthetic mode, there was a different and, perhaps, deeper criticism of liberalism. There was a simultaneous emergence of postindustrialism and poststructuralism.

The present change moves, I believe, to a still more profound sociocultural alteration as the context within which theory and research in sociology of education changes. Beyond the powerful effects of historic social movements in the first, political phase and the pervasive effects of a change in the societal mode of production and social organization in the second, aesthetic phase, I suggest that what the emergent religious phase augurs is a profound and not easily reversible change of direction in basic civilization assumptions.

Politics

The work of the seventies was a critique of the abstracted decontextualization and personal alienation of positivist sociology of education in which professional sociologists were sometimes so absorbed in solving particular research problems that they lost sight of their place within the broader framework of knowledge. Sociologists, busy with investigations, forgot their critical self-awareness and ignored the social meaning of their own intellectual problem-solving relative to everyday, practical living. In this phase of the 1970s, the goal was instead to place research in the sociology of education within a broader political context (Wexler, 1976:5). As I argued then, the sociology of education had centered on three issues: the relationship of education to social equality; the description and analysis of the social organization of schools; and the study of knowledge in the educational process. Underlying these concerns could be seen the ideals of Progressive-liberalism: equality as meritocracy, bureaucracy for social efficiency, and faith in scientific knowledge.

The critiques of prevalent modes of action and thought that originated in the events of the sixties became intellectualized, rationalized and made respectable in the language of the academic disciplines. But, in the 1970s, there was also dissent, critique, a demand for self-awareness and an attempt to develop a new model better able to integrate the social experiences and aspirations neglected or derided by earlier approaches (Wexler, 1976:7,8).

The political approach simultaneously addressed the practice of contextualizing research and the socially motivated emergence of new interests and assumptions for the field, which I called an "alternative" sociology of education (Wexler, 1976:54,55). I tried to connect academic research to culture and politics. In the sociology of education, a serious beginning was also made toward a set of new research emphases. The relationship between education and social inequality began to be studied by means of institutional relationships as well as individual characteristics. There was interest in the contextual and historical study of schooling. The political environment of educational organizations was made more explicit. The content of schooling was understood as the outcome of social processes rather than as the natural emanation of objective truth (Wexler, 1976:54,55).

This acculturated Kuhnianism was not only an entree to politicizing the method and content of academic work in the sociology of education, but also the door to a much wider horizon of Marxist thought that had been long absent from American academic discourse. The interest in meaning and alienation found more general expression in the psychocultural critiques of the so-called Hegelian Marxism of the Frankfurt School, Georg Lukacs, Antonio Gramsci and others. The effect was the establishment of a legitimating tradition and genuine resource for theoretical work in a powerfully empiricist sociological specialty.

The work of the eighties elaborated this new theoretical and political sociology of education, representing the alienation interest in terms of "reification," "ideology," and, especially, "commodification" applied to education. In *Social Analysis of Education* (Wexler, 1987), I tried to show how the political interest led to an emphasis on textuality, discourse, and signification as the new locus for dealienation through the demystification of the construction of meaning. I chided so-called new sociologists for their newfound legitimacy and failure to take critical theory more deeply into Romanticism, structuralism, and particularly the poststructuralist analyses that I argued were part of the discursive production emphasis of a postindustrial, complexly commodified society.

My critique of the not-so-new sociology of education was about what I have referred to here as the routinization and decadence of its successful challenge to liberal positivism. Marxist and critical ethnographies had abandoned the virtues of traditional anthropological organicism without yet appreciating a new contextualism that could guard against slippage into realist objectivism. The analogue to the decadence of qualitative organicism to variable analysis was the routinized degeneration of critical theoretical concepts into decontextualized categorical incantations, such as "class, race, and gender."

Aesthetics

These early poststructuralist interests were political:

> Post-structuralism brings the labor of signification to the surface, out from the suppressive weight of humanism's essentialist and substantialist reifications. It asserts the formative, active role of symbolic processes. That is one sense in which post-structuralism is, even against some of its own claims, a discourse directed toward a critical social practice: bringing symbolic processes to awareness and then to the active and creative possession of intentional practice. (Wexler, 1987:147)

The rightward corporatist movement that then was already described within postindustrialism, intensified in the educational sector. I described poststructuralism as a dereifying and dereified discourse. It could enable understanding of symbolic practice as the dominant, discursive mode of production and avoid the opaque, stereotypical theories and methods that emerged in the later, successful political phase of sociology of education. Poststructuralism became postmodernism. And postmodernism became a resignation, however ironic, oblique and displaced, to the language and practices of the culture of corporatist postindustrialism.

The critical theory tradition that had become the intellectual base of the field at the peak of its political phase was supplanted by a postmodern theory. Its quest for meaning encompassed a desire for dealienation. But, it also represented an acceptance of commodification's aestheticization of social life in a superficial, depoliticized, aesthetic word.

In education at least, social theoretical work went directly from the "radical" negation of the certain-knowledge/happy-life regime of the positive "mainstream" to a bibliophilic celebration of borrowed grand antitheories of postmodernism. I have argued that theories belonging to a decadent and disintegrative cultural phase, when they are not simply masquerading as traditional liberal pluralism, may be antithetical or reactionary to cultural context. Neither the historically important negation of critical theory, nor the more doubtful aestheticization of postmodernism and poststructuralism, succeeded in providing a fundamentally different alternative to the regime of positivity that they claimed to negate or dissolve. That requires going beyond critical theory and postmodernism more deeply into the culture's alternatives, toward a more general sociology of presence.

Chapter Three

Social Theory: Precursors and Subtexts

Sociology of Presence

We begin to construct a sociology of presence first through a rereading of social theory from a strategic vantage point that identifies the precursory elements of a new synthesis. As the transition out of Puritan, Enlightenment sociology is described within a cultural movement, this new synthesis is seen as part of a wider cultural process, which requires some brief description; the culture that feeds emergent academic theory is itself part of a new historical age. In such new circumstances, and with a strategic rereading of social theory, I begin to outline the basic interests and direction of a sociology that goes beyond representation of the transition called "postmodernism" into a new age. Ultimately, I explore what such a transfigured social theory might mean for a social theory and practice of education—and why a postmodern or poststructuralist approach is inadequate to the emerging social formation.

In the last 75 years, each generation has had its version of "classical sociology." But I don't think that we have yet had ours, unless the American cultural revolt of the sixties is going to count as a mature statement, rather than as either the expression of an earlier generation of sociologists, or as a preliminary voice of this one. The politicized, so-called radical reading of sociology never undid the postwar positivist, progressive Enlightenment, anti-Marxist interpretation of the sociological pillars.

The strategy with which I read now is to surpass the critical analysis that once helped to defend against the long shadow of the 1950s. That critical social analysis attacked pretenses to indifferent, antiseptic, certain, ritually secured knowledge, and behind that, to what Alvin Gouldner aptly called its "background assumptions" about the good and happy life. Critical social analysis was a negation, an opposition to an ahistorical, decultured sociology and to its denial of widespread social inequality, poverty and alienation. It was indeed a "hermeneutic of suspicion," as Paul Ricouer characterized critical theory—a suspicion of scientistic and moral pretenses in the face of the evident suffering of impoverishment and unhappiness, public corruption and the distortion of private lives.

Critical social analysis pulled the rug from what had been swept under it: not simply inequality and exploitation, but commodification of all social spheres and its most general human effect in the stultification of human potential, or, more broadly, "alienation." Marxism (and its tributaries) was the main theoretical resource for the New Left, sociological generational negation. Methodologism and social conservatism successfully claimed Emile Durkheim and Max Weber, while depth psychologies and secular and religious existential philosophies were cordoned off to a highbrow, though marginalized, general culture beyond the pale of social theory.

There has not been a strong or coherent tendency toward an "affirmative negation," one that is simultaneously a rejection of the falsely naturalized world of commodification, extreme rationalization, and its analogous culture of scientific rationalism—and the establishment of an ideal state of individual and collective being. Of course, academic Western Marxism wanted to make that claim. But history has shown what the dissenting cultural edge of the New Left suspected: that even the utopian critics and avatars of negation were unable to break through the social-psychological formations of repression that limited not only the character of their hopes for "liberation," but also the conceptual paths by which to grasp the present and to transform it. Both the conception of the negating critique and the forms of life that drove it only went part of the way, analytically demystifying the naturalized repressive social order without reaching and unleashing another form of life and the social understandings carried within it.

Here I have argued that postmodernism is a cultural sign of a disintegrative phase of positivity's regime. Further, after it, but already within it, a new culture emerges that carries socially transformative hopes over the boundaries that repression formerly set for them. This new culture means new ideals and also new ways of thinking about social and individual life. In its reflective aspect, traditions are brought forward and renewed, precursors and antecedents are rediscovered. Those precursors are in the cultural revolts of the sixties and seventies, and in the incipient social analyses that diagnosed the repression to be overcome, but were still unable to live and think beyond that regime's hegemony. (That is why, for example, I described "new sociology of education" as bound to the mainstream that it criticized.) The antecedents are not only in the culture and critical social thought of the sixties and seventies, or, ultimately, in the great core world civilizations, but also in the turn-of-the-century sociological cannon.

The new culture is the culture of the new age. Its ideal state is one that Erich Fromm referred to in his introduction to T.B. Bottomore and Maximilien Rubels' (1956) Marx reader as "de-alienation." This state or ideal of being is the driving point not only for Marx, but also for Durkheim and Weber. Dealienation involves in every case the collective production or release of socially bound energies that in their unrealized condition are the source of individual and collective distortion, disease, and historical blockages to the realization of higher evolutionary potentials. For the radical or left Freudians like Wilhelm Reich and Erich Fromm, and for the sociological existentialists like Martin Buber, the overcoming of socially organized alienation and repression releases collective energies that become reorganized as new modes of individual and collective being.

Postmodernism has not, however pervasive its practical mass and elite reflective cultures have been, succeeded in obliterating the drive to overcome alienation. That drive does however now take a different direction, just as the character of alienation has progressively deepened beneath the postmodern smoke screen of postindustrial, global capitalism. Both the disease and the cure are now more extreme.

The deformations of alienation that modernist analysts from Marx onward described, when they meant more than the appropriation of social agency or control and power, referred largely to destructive aspects of industrial labor. Of course, as Bertell Ollman (1971) and Fromm (1976) describe, the Marxist theory included also a premodern sense of "the more you have, the less you are." But for the later Marx—and indeed for Marxism more generally—the central interest was less in alienation and more in the social appropriation of labor, in exploitation, and in collective reappropriation of objectivized labor and property by an organized labor or producers movement.

The aspect of alienation that has deepened as industrialism has been followed by postindustrialism and modernism by postmodernism is that beyond the loss of agency there has been a loss of organic sensation, of feeling, and of being alive. While, like alienation theory in its labor, power, agency aspect, the vantage point of loss may represent a premodern sensibility, postmodernism has brought about a new drive toward the reversal of alienation in its very glorying in "deaths" of all kinds, including the organic death of being. Among the sociological high moderns, Max Weber described this organic effect, in the Romantic tradition, as "mechanical petrification."

It is this penetration of alienation to the organic level, to the petrification of life energy and the inducement of a certain life-inertness, that has encouraged a counterforce in what I believe is a new coalescence and configuration in social theory. This new direction in social theory is not an abstraction from wider cultural tendencies, any more than was postmodernism. The direction of a new social theory is toward social renewal. It builds on the variegated cultural resources of sociocultural trends that are simplistically lumped together as "new age." It is a counterforce or reaction to postmodern legitimation of the implosion of being or "mechanical petrification," or alienation, particularly in the sense of seeking revitalization of the experience of organic, bodily being. This apparent narcissism is a collective reassertion of the life force against a postmodern culture of death.

While it may begin at an organic, bodily level, the counterdrive soon discovers the social and cultural construction of being, and therefore seeks meaning. The channel for this search for being and meaning has been cleared of modernist blockages by postmodernism's function as destroyer of modern culture. Whether it is a premodern reversion, or as I think, a going beyond postmodernism to a new renaissance or renewal, the movement toward revitalization increasingly occurs within a cultural tendency toward resacralization (Thompson, 1990).

Revitalization movements and resacralization processes are complex, and multiple and contradictory in their effects. Nevertheless, I claim, following Pitirim Sorokin's early model (1957), that they are part of a broad cultural, civilizational shift. Sorokin predicted the shift toward an ideational cultural premise, following the decadence of a materialist senate culture. I am going to explore instead the emergence of a new age social theory within the context of a new age culture. Alienation, in this view, is not overcome by socialism, but through a resacralization-driven radical redirection of cultural and individual energies, which in turn leads to new social forms. As Weber argued in his analysis of charisma, which he called the "creative, revolutionary force of history": "Charismatic belief revolutionizes men 'from within' and shapes material and social conditions to its revolutionary will" (1968:1117,1116).

New Age Social Theory

Resacralization of culture will, I think, increasingly dissolve modernist and postmodernist sociologies alike back into core cultural traditions. Sociology, as a secular cosmology, is already being reintegrated with wider cultural movements. Its historic role as a secular cosmology and as a fulcrum between religious cultural traditions (the sacred) on the one side and commodity fetishism of everyday life (the profane) on the other becomes less salient within the current forms of social revitalization and renewal movements.

Simultaneously, new psychologies, particularly from cognitive paradigms, have worked their way toward theories of individual revitalization. For example, under the heading of adult play, "reversal theory" in cognitive psychology (Kerr and Apter, 1991), "Eastern religion" describes accomplishing a valued state of non-instrumental action:

> Eastern religions . . . suggest that only in the paratelic state can we experience the real nature of being, thus experience enlightenment. In grasping for goals outside ourselves, or being purposive and directive and determined, we miss the essence of what it is to be us. We cease to be mindful of the direct experience of

> living, and become caught up in the strivings which, though highly productive in one sense, risk desensitizing us to the present moment, which is ultimately all we have. (Fontana, 1991 in Kerr and Apter:160)

This cognitive psychological interest represents both the desire to overcome alienation and the wider current means of overcoming alienation through a renewal in which resacralization also encompasses the human sciences. The most well known exemplar of this work is Mihaly Csikszentmihalyi (1990, 1993). Under the banner of a "psychology of optimal experience," Csikszentmihalyi has been increasingly explicit that his research and theory is about overcoming alienation and, more recently, that focused states of attention, which he calls "flow," require contextualization in wider systems of meaning. A psychology that analyzes experience that is "beyond boredom and anxiety," the unalienated state of being, has been extended in that work to an evolutionary theory of being that is critically, but consciously, aligned both with new age culture and with pantheistically oriented religious traditions.

Csikszentmihalyi develops a theory of individual energy ("attention") that he links to new age movements and to "spiritual activity": "What is common to all forms of spirituality is the attempt to reduce entropy in consciousness" (1993: 239). Beginning from a very specific empirical research base, he has moved to an evolutionary, ecological ethic. Psychology becomes a vehicle for overcoming the deeper, postmodern form of the alienation of being through an ideal of cultural revitalization.

The social theory of the new age, then, is always, finally, beyond negation—theorizing, as Norman O. Brown put it, "the way out," surpassing repressed, commodified, rationalized social existence to the attainment of an ideal state of "nirvana" (Marcuse, 1955); "resurrection" (Brown, 1959); "orgasmic potency" (Reich, 1949); "acosmic brotherliness" (Weber, 1946); or a feminist-inspired "intersubjective mutuality" (Benjamin, 1988). While it takes multiple forms, there is an underlying common commitment to a theory of social energy, an energy that is biopsychological, but collectively shaped, inhibited and released. The generation of this energy, whether as "libido" or "bion," "effervescence" or "charisma," has its primal force in cultural creation, but particularly, in the religious experience and articulation at the fount of culture and society.

New age social theory is concerned with: the conditions for the creation and freeing of this social energy; the description of its precise character; how it works at the collective and individual levels; the processes of its regeneration and flow; its meaning and linkage in body, mind and soul; and, in a return to the initial "dealienated state," how social energy either leads to, or is inhibited from, paths of redemption, salvation and a messianic time that is beyond the regime of positivity, beyond the intense struggling phase of negation, and beyond the decadent phase of dissolution. New age social theory aims to imagine and realize optimal being in everyday social life. Education, while it is now at the pinnacle of a technocratic movement, is the site for the clearest articulation of new age social theory. In part, that is because education works through identity or self, which is now the central locus of a cultural transformation into a new age.

Precursors

This interest in an optimal state of being that is culturally generated and rooted in religion is hardly novel to the new age. My reading of Durkheim and Weber, against the positivist grain, suggests that they anticipated precisely this set of transformative interests. Although Durkheim is typically taught as the exemplar of scientific rationalism in sociology and as an exponent of individualism, his later essays make clear that "the cult of the individual" is a compromise with individualism, a compromise designed to favor collective ritual and not individualism. The "cult of the individual" is a transitional commitment, an acknowledgment of the end of the old order, and an extraction of all that is valuable in a more centrifugal society.

Durkheim's hope, however, is evidently not for his time of "moral cold," but for a "warmer" social existence, in which a collective religion energizes the moral life, which in turn enables both generative collective representation and the motivational discipline required for a restrained balancing of what are otherwise unlimited individual passions. Robert Bellah (1973) notably reads the passionate Durkheim, one who views collective energy and religion as the crux of social and individual life. Bellah writes of Durkheim:

> Repeatedly during his later years he hopes for a revival of the profound collective experience, the experience of fusion and ecstasy, which is the essence of primitive religion and the

> womb out of which the renewal of society at any period can take place. (1973:xlvi)

And further on, Bellah adds:

> In Durkheim there is to be found a moral vision, *a return to the depths of social existence* [emphasis added], which is in some ways more radical than that of his rivals. There are some significant parallels with Freud, since Durkheim was trying to understand the unconscious sources of social existence as Freud was the unconscious sources of personal existence. (1973:liv)

From our vantage point, Durkheim is not a "happy" modern, but rather one who anticipates the dawning of a new culture, a new age. What gives this anticipatory hope interpretive power is Durkheim's understanding of society as a field of forces, of creative social energy generated in the religious origins of collective life. On a new age, he wrote:

> The old ideals and the divinities which incarnate them are dying because they no longer respond sufficiently to the new aspirations of our day; and the new ideals which are necessary to orient our life are not yet born.
>
> But who does not feel—and this is what should reassure us—who does not feel that, in the depths of society, an intense life is developing which seeks ways to come forth and which will finally find them . . . a center of crystallization for new beliefs. (quoted in Bellah, 1973:xlvii)

In Durkheim's language of explanation for collective life, underlying images of cold and heat, there is a view of currents of energy and forces. This social energy is generated in religious activity, and it is the renaissance of such activity, which incurs the new age:

> In a word, the old gods are growing old or already dead, and others are not yet born. . . . A day will come when our societies will know again those hours of creative effervescence, in the course of which new ideas will arise. (Bellah, 1973:xlvii)

Against moral "stagnation," Durkheim looks toward the "spiritual" as the "ways that social pressure exercises itself" (Bellah, 1973:171). Religion is a "force" for occasions of "strengthening and *vififying* [emphasis added] action of society." There is a reciprocal flow of energy between individual and collective that is most evident during states of social effervescence. For the individual, at such times "he feels within him an abnormal over-supply of force which overflows and tries to burst out from him . . . this exceptional increase of force is something very real" (1973:173). Further, in the same section of *The Elementary Forms of the Religious Life*, he notes, significantly:

> But it is not only in exceptional circumstances that this stimulating action of society makes itself felt; there is not, so to speak, a moment in our lives when some *current of energy* [emphasis added] does not come to us from without. . . . this is the moral conscience, of which, by the way, men have never made even a slightly distinct representation except by the aid of religious symbols. (1973:174)

And again, the religious basis of social energy: "the forces that move bodies as well as those that move minds have been conceived in a religious form" (1973:186). So as to leave no doubt about the primacy of religion in a social life based in currents of energy, Durkheim declared in the journal L' Annee Sociologique:

> This year, as well as last, our analyses are headed by those concerning the sociology of religion. The according of the first rank to this sort of phenomenon has produced some astonishment, but it is these phenomena which are the germ from which all others—or at least almost all others—are derived. Religion contains in itself the very beginning, even if in an indistinct state, all the elements which in dissociating themselves from it, articulating themselves and combining with one another in a thousand ways, have given rise to the various manifestations of collective life. . . . At any rate, a great number of problems change their aspects completely as soon as their connections with the sociology of religion are recognized. (1960:350-1)

If religion is the primordial source of ideas, of collective representations, it is only because it is the source of social energy. Of the religious source of energy, he writes:

> To consecrate something it is put in contact with a source of religious energy, just as today a body is put in contact with a source of heat or electricity to warm or electricize it; the two processes are not essentially different. Thus understood, religious technique seems to be a sort of mystic mechanics. (in Bellah, 1973:192)

The language of mechanical energy is more than a convenient metaphor:

> in fact, we have seen that if collective life awakens religious thought on reaching a certain degree of intensity, it is because it brings about a state of effervescence which changes the conditions of psychic activity. Vital energies are over-excited. (1973:195)

Although Durkheim now may be seen as having been an opponent of Henri Bergson and his vitalist thought, the power of society for Durkheim is that "it is life itself" which has "a creative power which no other observable being can equal" (1973:222).

Weber also felt the necessity of a new age, but tentatively and with a deeply reserved sense of anticipation. For Weber too, religion is the source of social energy. Compared to Durkheim, his language and social analysis is less recontextualized to either a secular or more abstract and general theoretical plane. He is openly working out the sociocultural and individual consequences of various paths of religious action. His observations are historical, and the determinative social force of religion is culturally specific and full of unforeseen—and in the case of Puritan Protestantism, undesirable—cultural and individual effects. Religion may be the basic force. With characteristic ironic understatement, Weber wrote: "The modern man is in general, even with the best will, unable to give religious ideas a significance for culture and national character which they deserve" (1958a:183).

Yet, despite the contradictory social effects of the rationalization of magic to prophetic religions, the early rationalization of religious activity, "demagification," leads to the deadening closure of bureaucracy. This is the social organizational apparatus of a rationalized culture that destroys culture, produces only ersatz or fake prophecies, and dead-ends by locking the original creative energies of religion into an "iron cage."

The culture of the present age links its collective religious origins with a deformed, alienated individual way of life or social character:

> To-day the spirit of religious asceticism—whether finally, who knows?—has escaped from the cage. But victorious capitalism, since it rests on mechanical foundations, needs its support no longer. The rosy blush of its laughing heir, the Enlightenment, seems also to be irretrievably fading, and the idea of duty in

> one's calling prowls about in our lives like the ghost of dead religious beliefs.(1958:181-182)

"Mechanism" and the deadness of a "rationalist way of life" leads to the "personality type of the professional expert," who supplants "the cultivated type of man"(1958:240). In terms directly reminiscent of Marx's description of alienated being, Weber explains the consequences of the "mechanization and discipline of the plant" as those in which:

> the psycho-physical apparatus of man is completely adjusted to the demands of the outer world, the tools, the machines—in short, to an individual 'function'. The individual is shorn of his natural rhythm as determined by the structure of his organism. (1958:261-262)

And, in the "universal rationalization and intellectualization of culture . . . the total being of man has now been alienated from the organic cycle of peasant life" (1946:344). The social apparatus of bureaucratic specialization, which increases precision, speed, calculability and profit, also destroys the "cultivated man," and deadens or "petrifies" life in an "iron cage."

Weber's new age is a nebulous possibility because rationalization, for whatever scientific clarity it has brought—which he defends in "Science as a Vocation" (1946) against romantic academic ideologizing—has destroyed the spirit, which is the wellspring of cultural life:

> No one knows who will live in this cage in the future, or whether at the end of this tremendous development entirely new prophets will arise, or there will be a great rebirth of old ideas and ideals, or, if neither, mechanized petrification, embellished with a sort of convulsive self-importance. For the last stage of this cultural development, it might well be truly said: "Specialists without spirit, sensualists without heart; this *nullity* [emphasis added] imagines that it has attained a level of civilization never before achieved." (1958:182)

Against the life-destroying petrification of social mechanization in rationalized specialization, there is an antipodal force that has asserted itself historically to "transcend the sphere of everyday economic routines" (1968:111). That is "charisma," the "strongest anti-economic force" that "transforms all values and breaks all traditional and rational norms" (1968:115). Against rationalization, charisma is a specifically creative revolutionary force of history that depends not on office or juridical expertise. The revolutionary force is instigated from within experience and alters material and social conditions to fulfill charismatic purposes.

Like Durkheim's model of social energy in the dynamic density of "collective effervescence," charisma "arises from collective excitement produced by extraordinary events and from surrender to heroism of any kind" (1968:112). But charisma is inherently unstable because of the "desire to transform charisma and charismatic blessing from a unique, transitory gift of grace of extraordinary times and persons into a permanent possession of everyday life."

Despite the inevitable instability of charisma and the flourishing of ersatz prophecy, Weber does seek a way out of the iron cage by a reexamination of asceticism and mysticism (1946: 323-59). Asceticism tends toward rationality and is sublimated in knowledge. Mysticism, with its emphasis on unity and ecstasy, has "always inclined men towards the flowing out into an objectless acosmism of love. . . . But its ethical demand has always lain in the direction of universal brotherhood" (1946:330). This tendency conflicts with the other sociocultural spheres of aesthetics and eroticism. These spheres, which are "like a gate into the most irrational and thereby *real kernel of life,* [emphasis added] as compared with the mechanisms of rationalization," are in tension with the "ethic of religious brotherliness."(1946:345) Ultimately though, it is the "vocational workaday life, asceticism's ghost, which leaves hardly any room" for "the cultivation of acosmic brotherliness" (1946:357).

Charisma, grace and gratitude, magic, spirit, ecstasy, care and love were harnessed by intellectualization in prophecy and rationalization in an ever more centralized, specialized, scientific and precisely calculable social apparatus. Yet, despite the unintended deadening effects of the disenchantment and demagification of the world, the irrational, real kernel of life struggles for reappearance on the collective historical stage as the revolutionary spirit of a personal grace that, like Durkheim's effervescence, flows between the individual and the collective as excitement of "particular states." "Pianissimo," in everyday life, the mystical drive toward union and ecstasy and its implied ethic of an acosmic love struggle, in an inner tension with aestheticism and eroticism, to reclaim the force or energy of "the transformation from within."

Charismatic energy, ecstasy and love are the life that is opposed to the apparently triumphant death entailed in "mechanized petrification." Either through the fusion of energy in mystical union, or through its diffusion in caring or 'caritas' (interpersonal) love, there are ways out, though they are, in Weber's early twentieth-century world, inaccessible, "unless it is among strata who are economically carefree" (1946:357).

Mid-twentieth-century social thought continues to articulate the conflict between a deadening civilization and life-affirming cultural and personal forces. Yet, this articulation is found less within either mainstream or radical sociology or in rationalized postmodernism. Instead, it is found in the work of religious existentialists like Martin Buber and dissident theorists and practitioners of psychoanalysis like Wilhelm Reich, Norman O. Brown, Erich Fromm and others (Marcuse, 1955; Benjamin, 1988).

Brown derives the struggle of "life against death" not from the combination of Georg Simmel's sociology of urban alienation and Jewish mysticism as we shall see with Martin Buber, but from a Romantic, Christian reinterpretation of Freud's "libido" as more a life force than, in Freud's terms, a "love force." The alienated state is repression, and, Brown writes:

> Therefore the question confronting mankind is the abolition of repression—in traditional Christian language, the resurrection of the body. (1959:307)

In opposition to Freud, who saw repression as an individual and civilizational necessity, Brown calls for the elimination of all repression, in a liberation of the body: "The life instinct also demands a union with others and with the world around us based not on anxiety and aggression but on narcissism and erotic exuberance" (1959:307).

Brown also looks to religion, particularly Western mysticism, as a channel through which repression/alienation can be overcome. "So seen," he writes, "psychoanalysis is the heir to a mystical tradition which it must affirm"(1959:310). Mysticism and Romanticism (the latter of which Freud did acknowledge as the precursor to his theory of the unconscious) "stays with life," and surpasses the critical negation of analysis with affirmation of "the spiritual," energetic and perfectible body:

> Modern poetry, like psychoanalysis and Protestant theology, faces the problem of the resurrection of the body. Art and poetry have always been altering our ways of sensing and feeling—that is to say, altering the human body. And Whitehead rightly discerns as the essence of the "Romantic Reaction" a revulsion against abstraction (in psychoanalytical terms, sublimation) in favor of the concrete sensual organism, the human body. (1959:312)

Brown then quotes the poet, William Blake: "Energy is the only life, and is from the Body. . . . Energy is eternal Delight"(1959:312).

The return of the concrete, the body as the locus of energy, and its deeper source in mystical religion, all lead to a view of social theory itself as part of the apparatus of repressive alienation or, in this language, neurosis of civilization:

> Contemporary social theory (again we must honor Veblen as an exception) has been completely taken in by the inhuman abstractions of the path of sublimation, and has no contact with concrete human beings, with their concrete bodies, their concrete though repressed desires, and their concrete neuroses.(1959:318)

For Reich, the dealienation or undoing of the repressed body is not a mystical, but a material, "vegetative system" process that can be experimentally traced to the cellular or "bion" level. Psychoanalytic work in the "talking" therapy led him first to a recognition of the embodiment of neurosis in the entire musculature in a process of defense against anxiety that creates "armor" which is fully physical as well as psychological. This armor binds and blocks and dams up the natural flow of bio-energy, causing deformation and disease. The natural flow of energy is realized through, following the Freudian model of psychosexual development, the expression of genitality, in orgasmic sexual interaction (Reich, 1949).

In Reich's theory, full genitality makes transparent the flow or "streamings" of body energy that are repressed in character armors that ultimately derive from the social pathologies of an authoritarian, patriarchal, antisexual, repressive social order. By understanding both "sex-pol," the sociopolitical formation of sexuality, and the sex-economy of body and interpersonal energy dynamics, a genitality of the unrepressed streamings releases body energy for individual and collective creative self-transformation. Edward Mann and Edward Hoffman (1980) recount the development of Reich's work, from radical sex-pol psychoanalysis to a holistic body therapy of energy and then simultaneously toward a more materialist theory of energy field in self and environment on the one hand, and toward a more religious or, as they describe it, "spiritual reawakening", on the other.

Reich is an important precursor, although he stands quite outside the sociological canon. His energy theory represents a therapeutic and political commitment to an dealienated state and to a social psychology of presence. Social pathology is represented in individual psychology and biology. The biodynamics of the body offer a dealienated state from which to counter repression, first at the individual interactive, sex-therapeutic, holistic health level, and then, from there, in a broader social reform, especially through sex education, but also in a model of self-regulation of children (A. S. Neill of Summerhill fame was a disciple of Reich). If it is Romanticism, it is of a materialist, even experimental variety. Like the classical sociologists, for Reich, energy is real, culturally shaped and individually embodied. Toward the end of his life, it appears that "the way out" (although in fact there was none for him; Reich died in prison in Lewisburg, Pennsylvania) recognized an interaction of the spheres of the body, mind, social organization and spirituality as the path both of understanding and of practice by which life energies could overcome the socially induced living death that Reich repeatedly observed in his clinical practice and his social critics. Like Brown, Reich saw the purpose of practice and analysis as the resurrection of life against a culture of death.

Subtext: Sorokin

The quest for a sociology of presence with an analytical interest in a theory of social energy and a transformative interest in a life-affirming practice is a strong Romantic thread that runs through classical sociology, psychoanalysis, and existentialism. But, the social theorist who most self-consciously heralds a new age and tries to derive its arrival empirically and theoretically stands outside of West European Romanticism: Pitirim Sorokin.

Sorokin's analysis of social and cultural dynamics (1957) is a phase or wave theory of European civilization. Empirically, cultural and social forms are characterized in a chronological periodization of sensate, ideational and idealist cultures. Each culture has its own mentality that structures all the predominant social forms and values. There is a certain tendency to coherence in cultural systems and an immanent evolution in a system reaching its limit and beginning a disintegrative phase. The two types of polar cultures are the ideational and the sensate. Ideational culture assumes an ultimate supersensate, immaterial, spiritual reality. As Sorokin puts it, "In brief, the Sensate culture is the opposite of the Ideational in its major premises" (1957:28).

The first part of Sorokin's encyclopedic cultural inventory is a classification of cultures and a discussion of subtypes, as well as the rules of integration and the disintegrative succession of mentalities. The second part is a diagnosis of "the crisis of our age," which is, of course, for Sorokin, the decline of the 600-year-old wave of the sensate culture, and the emergence of either an ideational or an idealistic culture. We are now living, he wrote in the thirties, in a painful transitional stage in which the sensate culture is dying.

> We are seemingly between two epochs: the dying Sensate culture of our magnificent yesterday, and the coming Ideational or Idealistic culture of the creative tomorrow. We are living, thinking, acting at the end of a brilliant six-hundred year-long sensate day (1957:625). Sensate culture is now "in agony": when through its achievements it has given into man's hands terrific power over nature and the social and cultural world, without providing himself with self-control . . . it is becoming increasingly dangerous (1957:628).

A sensate culture cannot provide that because of its expedient and hedonistic character. As a result, we are "at the end of the road," although there is a slow emergence of an alternative. Interestingly, Sorokin's description of the current phase of sensate culture seems apt for postmodernism, with its "syncretism of undigested elements, devoid of a unity or individuality." The crisis precedes an ensuing catharsis of suffering, by which culture will be "brought back to reason, and to eternal, lasting universal, and absolute values." This suffering is, in Sorokin's terms, followed by a period of charisma and resurrection, and the "release of new creative forces" (1957:702).

If we are at such a transitional time, alternate cultural premises appear in the bazaar, including those that call for a rejection of the mechanist philosophy of the Enlightenment in favor of a revived, holistic vitalism. Only during such a time should we expect a revival of interest in Henri Bergson and a reader on the crisis in modernism (Burwick and Douglass, 1992) that reexamines vitalism. In his essay on vitalism and contemporary thought, Joseph Chiari reasserts an anti-mechanistic life philosophy:

> In one form or another, whatever the name, some type of energy, essence, or "entelechy" of life cannot be done away with or declared dead, for it is inherent in life. . . . Life is above all becoming . . . the elan vital is creative freedom, in the image of God, not confined to the biosphere. . . . It is the dynamic energy which guides the evolution of the living. (1992:245-73)

At this level of generality, talk of a new cultural age is hypothetical and apparently removed from the traditions of empirical social science. What is, I think, interesting, is the extent to which survey analyses of the hegemonic, so-called baby-boom generation reveal at the concrete level of individual lives and opinions the same sort of shift in assumptions described by Sorokin. Notably, in his recent book Wade Clark Roof (1993) reports survey results on what he refers to as a "generation of seekers." According to Roof,

> They are still exploring, as they did in their years growing up; but now they are exploring in new, and, we think, more profound ways. Religious and spiritual themes are surfacing in a rich variety of ways—in Eastern religions, in evangelical and fundamentalist teachings, in mysticism and new age movements, in Goddess worship and other ancient religious rituals, in the mainline churches and synagogues, in Twelve Step recovery groups, in concern about the environment, in holistic health, and in personal and social transformation. . . . baby boomers have found that they have to discover for themselves what gives their lives meaning, what values to live by. (1993:4-5)

What Roof foresees for the nineties is a "reemergence of spirituality." Indeed, against the conventional wisdom of this as the political, radical generation, he observes: "The generation may well be remembered, in fact, as one that grappled hard in search of a holistic, all-encompassing vision of life and as a spiritually creative generation" (1993:243).

While there is a postmodernism in this pastiche-style of spirituality, it is also a search for post-material values, although the commitment to the search is through an emphasis on self. Indeed, like Norman O. Brown, Roof raises the possibility of a two-sided narcissism, in which baby-boomer narcissism is "compatible with the positive, reinforcing role of religion: a person's need for affirmation, for encouragement, for support, for expressiveness." He continues: "a transformed narcissism is not only compatible with a religious orientation but may well be crucial to the continuing role of the sacred in a secular society" (1993:258).

Roof's analysis indicates the existence of a resacralized scaling of life which seeks a "new vital balance of spirituality and social action" and creates new communities through a "far quieter rhetoric—that of the soul" (1993:260, 261). Additional support for these surveys appears in the best-seller lists, in which the traditional self-help literature now has as a best-seller a book on spiritual practices that calls for "the care of the soul" (Moore, 1992). At the same time, phenomenological psychologists, like Eugene Gendlin, also see narcissism's value in self and social transformation. As Gendlin asks: "Has experience now become a possible source of social criticism?" (1987:251).

New Age Education?

As we saw in a review of change in social theory and education, the academic changes lagged, but were deeply bound up with a set of wider cultural changes. Both radical theory and poststructural analyses were part of a broader cultural movement (Wexler, 1976, 1987).

I have not described here in any detail the full flowering of new age culture as the emergent mass culture. Rather, I have indicated a general theory of cultural change and tried to show that there is some evidence for a move toward a culture with a different set of assumptions than those that have prevailed since at least the Renaissance: less rationalist, scientific, materialist and mechanical, and instead, more spiritual, ideational, vitalist and transcendental.

In addition, I have argued that the sociological canon—particularly Durkheim and Weber, who have functioned to legitimate positivist sociology's methodologism and scientism—were already seekers of a new age, and that core elements of new age culture or social cosmology are represented in their theories. Reinforcing that tendency, I included under the rubric of social theory psychoanalytic theorists and existential philosophers who, by training, professional affiliation and social orientation, are social theorists as well. This Romantic stream, reexamined classical sociology, and new age cultural tendencies combine to provide the outlines of a new age social theory.

As a beginning, here I have focused on a commonly held interest in "energy" and in overcoming alienation that is defined across a wide spectrum, from an environmental electrical field, to bioenergy, to "holy sparks," as Buber calls the dynamic of truly interactive pedagogy. In each case, energy reaches back to some universal life-principle and forward to both social processes and the external formation and internal process of individual lives. How these different interpretations and dynamics congeal and work is, of course, a primary theoretical issue for any new age sociology or social cosmology and its practical social ethic, or practice, in therapy, education and everyday life.

While the religious dimension is also quite variable, it is crucial to each of these theories. At the very least, causally, as in Durkheim, religion is the primal channel of social energy that has its source in collective life itself. More forcefully, in Weber for example, religion is not only the major template for culture and society, intended or unintended, but also the dynamic principle of history, as charisma. Social goals are intermediaries of religious aspirations for salvation, and in a secular age, socioculturally revolutionary and practically redemptive paths are recontextualizations of religion. The problem of the old order, rationalization, is Puritan Protestantism gone awry, and its solution is an innerworldly mysticism gone interpersonal. While we may argue Weber's intention on this last point, in any case, hope for a new age is a hope for prophecy and the path for the renewal of culture is spiritual.

Weber's religious solutions are not fully confident. But whatever ambivalence may be attributed to Weber's approach to rationalism, it is indisputable that he struggled with every sphere of social existence to find what Brown calls a "way out" of the iron cage of life-destroying societal, cultural and personal rationalization. Ultimately, it is only by bringing what is otherworldly and opposed to mundane or economic existence into practical conduct through prophecy that Brown's desirable states of union and love can be realized.

"Love's body" is what Brown and Reich want, in an unrepressed embodiment that defines for them the ideal or dealienated state. Brown's body is Christian and mystical, while Reich's is reducible to "bions" and less the incarnation of spirit (although character armor, however physical, is a residue of interpersonal and not simply biochemical or "vegetative" relations) than of environmental fields of energy.

Energy, an ideal state beyond current alienation and repression, a culturally life-affirming and generative religiosity, and harbingers of a new historic age are the commonalities of these antecedents and beginnings. Further, there is also, certainly with Reich, but less noticeably perhaps in Weber, as well as incipiently in our other exemplary theorists, the outlines of a new language for social analysis, a language that is at once religious and spiritual, but also interpretively valuable for understanding or explanation: in other words, a new social cosmology that has a simultaneously analytical and practically transformative interest.

The main site of this work is, of course, not the churches, nor social movements in their articulated stages. Rather, the cultural and social transformation occurs first evidently as the "transformation from within," at the site of the self. Education in the new age is first and foremost necessarily self-centered. The debate about narcissism (Gendlin, 1987) is not a theoretical or even moral dispute. Rather it is about two sides of a social dynamic and its consequences. On one side, there is the contemporary emphasis on "the body," in social practice and increasingly, I think, in social theory. Any transformatively interested education for a new age will be about the body. Indeed education, as Michel Foucault and others (Gore, 1995) have shown, has always been about the body, disciplining and binding it into the social order.

New age body education is about our first principle, "energy," and the recovery and stimulation of life energy that has, as in Weber's "mechanical petrification," become inert. This education is about waking the body, the energy streamings, as Reich would have had it, from their death in life. Of course, the new age therapeutic apparatus involves this same interest. From a social psychological vantage point, such a new "triumph of the therapeutic" is a response to the need for a sense of human agency, which has been so far repressed interpersonally, culturally and macrosocially, that only at the biofeedback level can the alienated self reexperience itself.

Body education is not only a sign of defeat. It represents the stirring of a counterforce—"energy." But the dialectic of body education for the awakening and release of bioenergies is that it is energy regeneration for residual self-effectivity that has merely the consequence of producing more individual energy for incorporation and use by the petrified and petrifying social apparatus. Incorporation occurs not only into the apparatus, but also into unthinking cults of the new age. What begins as a stirring of bioenergy for self-social effectivity—which, of course, in actuality goes beyond the minimal, biological level—becomes reassimilated into cultural programs as diverse as twelve-step methods; evangelical, fundamentalist religion; and mass amalgamated reductions of psychoanalysis that use the apparatus to manipulate the unconscious electronically, rather than either mechanically or interpersonally.

What Weber understood was that while such activities of salvation may be enjoyable, the transformative possibility (which he called "revolutionary") is only realized when the release of energies (to now use our terms) is poured into the work of intellectualization. Without intellectualization, "experience," however altered, remains enjoyment, working in the unintended service of incorporation into the uncritical prevailing social apparatus and its new age counterposed cultures. The point is that a social theory–based education in a new age recognizes the need for the reintellectualization of released energies. It so becomes necessarily an education of the mind and not only of the body. What the new age cultural shift can offer, however, is the opening of alternative cultural resources for learning and thinking. By that, I don't mean simply multiculturalism, which aborts a more global awareness in favor of liberal accommodation.

The work of reintellectualization—education for the mind, of disciplined thought with wider cultural resources—points to the other side of narcissism, to why a self-centered education opens a third way, an alternative "way out," beyond the current polarity between consumption and production as the bases for educational thought and practice. Consumption, as Max Horkheimer and Theodor Adorno so trenchantly warned, leads to the amalgamation of thought with advertising(1972). Production, as we increasingly see, reduces thought to performance. And against the postmodernist philosopher Jean-Francois Lyotard, performance is not an opening to polyform inventiveness. In reality, the overwhelming tendency in educational reform is the dynamic that David Harvey (1989) has described as the regime of postindustrial flexible accumulation. As we have described it, educational reform is strongly corporatist and technocratic, redefining both the curriculum and the student/subject as aspects of performance/skills criteria. The issue is less appropriate curriculum content and more that the relation between subject or self and knowledge is itself collapsed, so that there is no distance between the performance/skill and the performer. Postindustrial definitions of education are centralizing, despite the rhetoric of "flexibility," and naturalize the self's disappearance into the performance.

On the other side of performance education stands the false opposition of postmodernism, which, despite its self-presentation of antinarrativity, is the metanarrative of consumption. It heralds decentralization and diffusion as a cultural strategy of self-destruction. Ultimately, postmodernism fuses itself, however ironically, to the consumer culture it periodically tries to escape. In that way, it fulfills Horkheimer and Adorno's (1972) warning about the incorporation of thinking into the logic of advertising, which is the lowbrow analogue to highbrow postmodern antirepresentational forms of representation. Even the irony, as a form of critique and way of maintaining distance against a crushing mass cultural apparatus, surrenders to the protest of ornamentalism, substituting marginal formalisms for self-affirming thinking that stops the tearful laughter of irony long enough for mindful creation.

Within the overarching cultural change, the educational tendencies are contradictory. On the one hand, there is narcissism and body education, with its dialectic of emancipatory though unsocialized possibility of meaning; on the other there is further, deeper organic petrification and commodification. The implications of body and indeed "soul" education remain largely at the theoretical and research level, with the exception of more traditional Gnosticism, which may be appropriated by rethinking movements like spiritually orientated Steiner schools. The main educational tendency, at least in the United States, is the corporatist productionist emphasis, in the public sector and in the restructuring of schools. A third possibility that now emerges is the need for a remoralized corporatism and a character or values education that is offered as a counterweight to the cultural negligence of the Toyota school corporatist restructuring of education.

The practical, educational effects of the cultural transformation that I am indicating—a transition well outside and beyond the emergent liberal binary of the economistic (corporatist) and culturalist (character education) program—are institutionalized only in the most fragmentary forms. Rather, both the economic and cultural liberal interests are forging educational change by a successful mobilization of broad-scale networks, while new age culture has been networked most successfully only in its commodified, commercial forms. Its transformative aspect remains local, body-centered and eclectic in its reintellectualization that is the necessary groundwork for legitimation and mobilization. This educational movement, which will provide a real alternative to the hegemonic binary of work/character, remains diffuse and uncrystallized at the larger network levels necessary for the means of collective mobilization now required for changing institutional practice.

A practical question for the future is whether changes in curriculum and pedagogy can be intellectually or theoretically derived from understandings of cultural and sociological changes, or whether meaningful discussion is only possible after practical institutional changes have begun to occur and these educational theories emerge as their reflexions. In either case, we are going to explore both paths: social analysis of incipient socioeducational movements—broadly conceived—of the new age, and theoretical implications of a new age social theory for education.

Recollection of the body for an energizing new age education can only resist feeding the electronic apparatus—which now regulates the unconscious by images—by reintellectualization, widening and deepening the life of the mind. Given the medium of religiosity, both in the contemporary cultural transformation and in the emergence of a social theory with practical implications for education, reminding will occur in the thrall of states of being that one moved, at least in American culture, William James, Walt Whitman and Ralph Waldo Emerson. Reintellectualization motivated by experienced values through religious states of being unavoidably recalls the language of spirit and soul.

New age culture is not merely about a twelve-step sort of interest in mass-produced programmed "recovery," but about a deeper recovery of the soul, a "return" or "turning" in Buber and Fromm's language. The recovery of the soul becomes then the transcendental polarity to the self-centered educative recollection of the body and its life energy. Fromm's theory of becoming can be read as a way of bringing the soul to life, although he still used secular, behavioral language in his struggle for dealienation.

New age culture spawns parallel methodologies, such as Thomas Moore's (1992) popular *Care of the Soul* and its sequels, which openly use the language of the soul and the sacred to describe the connection between transcendental being and cultural practices affecting individual lives. In a far cry from critical pedagogy, cultivation of the soul in a new age will call out to a teaching for transcendence—going beyond the critical social analysis that was Western humanism's Enlightenment heir, beyond the Romantic reaction and its vitalist history, to a new age in both social practice and social theory. I am tempted to conclude a discussion of new age social theory and education with Weber's observation that, "No one knows who will live in this cage in the future"(1958:182).

The Gilded Cage: An Example of Postmodern Sociology of Education

But now, we do know who will live in this cage: the postmodern bureaucrat. Not petrified, but supple; not monolithic and monotonous, but multivalent and polyvocal. The analytical voice of this historic figure becomes poststructuralism, applied self-defensively to the postmodern form of life, separated from whatever critical intentions held by the theoretical seers and precursors of postmodernity as a way of life and poststructuralism as an analytical orientation.

Perhaps the most interesting and self-aware example of this confluence applied to educational practice is represented by Ian Hunter's *Rethinking the School* (1994). Hunter brings a Foucauldian logic and language to his analysis of the school as a social institution. This logic, as Michel Foucault demonstrated early in his methodological "archaeology," and later in his genealogical studies (notably of the panoptic society) and ethics of the subject, "the relationship of self with self" (1990:6), is of a discontinuous history. It offers an incoherent configuration of social forms and practices and a contingent and fluid self.

Hunter's analysis of schooling is no less polemical than is Foucault's antihumanism, in the way he sets the historical, social, discursive study of school against the straw dog of "principled," moral absolutist approaches to education. These principled approaches posit school as an unfulfilled, incomplete realization of the ideal of reflective personal development—whether as the autonomous moral person of liberalism's democratic ideals or as the dialectical, collective monoperson of the working class. These principled studies are analytically blinded to the hybrid, contingent, and improvisational character of the assemblage of discursive social technologies as institutions. Instead of an effective history that can articulate unstable amalgams rather than represent blemished ideals as social historical accounts, we have had liberal and critical sociologies of education insensitive both to the centrality of social practices yoked to the bureaucratic governmentality of social training of populations for state citizenship as well as to their own ambiguous social position as exemplars of governmentally required moral discourse.

The school that Hunter describes is the educational element of a pastoral bureaucracy that appropriated a secularized Pietist pastoral pedagogy for reasons of an ascendant bureaucratic state's population management and training requisites. This is an historically contingent amalgam of social practices, an improvisation resulting from an historical scarcity of pedagogical technologies and the apparent effectiveness of pastoral methods for governmental purposes. Advocates of principled, moral accounts of schooling have ignored not only the central governmental role of education, but also the pastoral character of pedagogy, because they see schools as unfulfilled promises of development in relation to the self reflective person and of a morally warranted egalitarianism that results within a regime of collective political eschatology.

In my view, Hunter's contribution is manifold. The Foucauldian analysis of social institutions rescues us from the traditional organicism, abstracted individualism, and economic reductionism that continues to characterize the various mainstreams in the social analysis of education: functionalism, variable analysis, and neo-Marxism. The study of social practices enables a more specific, fine-grained institutional study that does not have to choose between cardboard representations of macro-structural themes and subjective narratives passing as micro-level representations of ethnography. Instead, there is a field of social practices, from which institutions like the school are assembled, by historically typified social actors for particular social purposes. Whatever its polemical motivation and framing, this analytic encourages a more differentiated, deanthropomorphized, tentative understanding of internal relations ("practices") and interinstitutional relations ("assemblages") that entertain the possibility of a profane, rather than "principled," sacred analysis of everyday social and educational institutions.

Hunter's contribution to the debate on schooling is to be found both in the particular hypothesis about the origins of European school systems and their current operation that he offers and in the analytical mode, strategy and language that he adapts from Foucault. The empirical focus on the transvaluative use of pastoralism by the bureaucratic state is a valuable corrective to a view in which schooling is only a vehicle for the production of class-shaped and differentiated labor power. The emphasis on state-production, and on pastoralism, opens up possibilities for the further study of schooling and of education more broadly.

To these solid contributions, Hunter adds the delightful bonus of a relentless invective against moralizing "critics." In *Social Analysis of Education* (1987), I tried to place the new sociology of education in an historical context, and to encourage the reflexive critics to become self-reflexive about their own work and social practice, as members of what I later referred to (self-inclusively) as the skeptical wing of the corporate, professional middle class. Hunter is more passionate. He is impatient with analysis besmirched by "political delusions" compounded by the hypocrisy of social withdrawal of critics who are integral, in their very pastoral "uppityness," to the contemporary apparatus.(1994: xi-xxiii) Here, Hunter's genealogy, through Foucault and Weber's common ancestor, Nietzsche, shows in his hatred of Christian morality and its agents, whatever secularized holiness they are provisionally clothed in as theorists and critics.

All this is to the good. In other words, let us praise practical, empirical criticism, deep revision and the renewal of social understanding against the sea of simultaneously complacent and fearful thinking and writing that passes for social analysis and criticism in education.

The "principled" educational criticism is normative, driven by a "should-be" delusional imposition of the secularized developmental ideals of Christian morality, rather than by a commitment to describing the origin and operation of schooling as a system of practical social technologies. Yet, I am not convinced by Hunter's empirical analysis of this actuality, either historically or contemporaneously.

At least for the American context, the claim that the school institution was the product neither of democratic politics nor of capitalist economics is not systematically sustained in Hunter's engaging governmental hypothesis. *Rethinking the School* lacks a careful review and rebuttal of alternative historical explanations. Even the American revisionists, whom one might prefer to classify as economic reductionists, had political interpretations of mediating formative processes between economy and school (Wrigley, 1982), emphasizing as Michael Katz did (1971) the importance of "bureaucracy" in the history of school formation. Perhaps more importantly, there is a lineage of American liberal educational historiography that antedates revisionism. Hunter participates in the revisionist myopia and fails to even entertain the complex discussion of democratic politics in the works of educational historians such as Lawrence Cremin (1961), Bernard Bailyn (1960), and Rick Welter (1962).

As for capitalist economics, the contemporary state, which I would much prefer to analyze in the language of the late Christopher Lasch as a "therapeutic state"—an American version of "pastoral bureaucracy" (wherein moral freedom and moral citizenship are coterminous)—is neither that nor a current administrative apparatus. Rather, "the state," in both narrow and wider senses of "governmentality," is increasingly an entrepreneurial state. *New York Times* writers are not enthusiastic about this transformation:

> Interrupting the nation's latest embrace of big business as being more efficient than big government, the bankruptcy of Orange County in California reminded Americans last week of what's at stake when inventive public officials blithely emulate private entrepreneurs—and lose. . . . The bankruptcy was a singular event, but raises profound and often forgotten questions about accountability and fairness as governments across the country mimic business by engaging in what is broadly hailed as privatization and public entrepreneurship. . . . "The greed sold to the need," said Dale Scott, a San Francisco investment adviser to governments. . . . (Roberts, 1994:1)

Using the administrative apparatus, with its hybridized social technology of pastoralism, as a model for understanding all institutional processes is put in question by the diffusion of the logic of the market as the exemplary practice for the operation of social assemblages.

Nor can "spiritual politics," as Hunter would have it, be assumed to have been superseded, its heirs found only in secular cloaks in an uneasy alliance with an apparently more neutral, less bloodthirsty administrative apparatus and its intellectuals. Rather, spiritual politics is the open partner of triumphant market logic, both in official state politics—as the rhetoric and results of recent U. S. elections demonstrate—and in the everyday micropolitics within the institutional networks. There is now serious discussion about returning prayer to public schools. Seventy percent of Americans believe in the existence of angels. Sublimated holiness in the moralizing criticisms of educational intellectuals is superfluous.

As Hunter exemplifies in his own arguments and in his polemics, however, critique is not superfluous—nor is social theory. Yet, despite Hunter's obvious and effective relish in using social theory for critical purposes, he is, I think, overanxious to cover his tracks and so denies the critical interests of his own theoretical foundations. Hardheaded, neutral, empirical realism and the call for actuality against delusional moralizers is a good stance, and, of course, the right social persona to assume for someone who would like to give administrative intellectuals their due in terms of the virtues of their own comportment. However, the theories that make Hunter's analysis possible, notably the works of Foucault and Weber, are not socially neutral, despite their insistence on more complex and differentiated sociohistorical analyses, and despite Hunter's forgetting this and presenting them as if they were.

Foucault is clearly a critic of the "carceral" society. In his words:

> the target nowadays is not to discover what we are, but to *refuse* [emphasis added] what we are. We have to imagine and to build up what we could be to get rid of this kind of political "double bind," which is the simultaneous individualization and totalization of modern power structures. . . . The conclusion would be that the political, ethical, social, philosophical problem of our days is not to try to liberate the individual from the state, and from the state's institutions, but to *liberate* [emphasis added] us both from the state and from the type of individualization which is linked to the state. We have to promote new forms of subjectivity through the refusal of this kind of individuality which has been imposed on us for several centuries. (1982:216)

Hunter is right that Foucault is antihumanist and opposed to universalizing ethics and analytical strategies. This does not mean that Foucault is not a critical theorist:

> "It seems to me that the philosophical choice with which we find ourselves confronted at present is this one: we can opt either for a critical philosophy presenting itself as analytical philosophy of truth in general, or for a critical thinking that takes the form of an ontology of ourselves or an ontology of the present. The latter form of philosophy, from Hegel to the Frankfurt School passing through Nietzsche and Max Weber, has founded a form of reflection in which I have tried to work." (Foucault as quoted in Hoy, 1986:22)

The uses of Weber are more unfortunate; not as a dispute in scholarship, but because the denial of Weber's profound critical, transformative interest works to legitimate both the avoidance of critical thought in the present and the critical/theoretical grounds of Hunter's argument. Of course, Weber recognizes the bureaucrat as an historically important social type, to be analyzed in its own terms, and, of course, Weber described differentiated social orders or "spheres," rather than a unidimensional social order. But, to conclude from that, as Hunter does, that "the professional comportment of the bureaucrat will lie beyond the ethical reach of its 'critical' problematization in an autonomous 'civic' domain" (1994:151), gives the appearance that Weber was, in the textbook interpretation, "value neutral" and, even further, applauded the bureaucratic apparatus and its agents.

In his later works, especially in the canonical essays on the sociology of religion, Weber not only criticized the emergent apparatus, but also desperately sought a "way out" of the new order that he described and analyzed. At the analytical level, recognition of different spheres does not obviate Weber's claim that there is a "universal rationalization and intellectualization of culture" (1946:344). Weber's distaste for the new social machinery pervades his work. What may be misleading is his refusal to find some simple way out, to take consolation in sacrificing scientific reason to ersatz prophecy. Of his critique, and of its basis in an ideal, there should be little doubt. If a reading of his 1916 essay "Religious Rejections of the World and Their Directions" (i.e. "ways out") fails to persuade one of Weber's interest in a "religious ethic of brotherliness," an intellectual struggle that appears as he works through the obstacles in each of the social spheres, then listen to what he writes about the "figures" of the new order:

> No one knows who will live in this cage in the future, or whether at the end of this tremendous development entirely new prophets will arise, or there will be a great rebirth of old ideas and ideals, or, if neither, *mechanized petrification* [emphasis added], embellished with a sort of convulsive self-importance. For of the last stage of this cultural development, it might well be truly said: "Specialists without spirit, sensualists without heart; this *nullity* [emphasis added] imagines that it has attained a level of civilization never before achieved."(1958:182)

To forget such critical ire is not an error of scholarship, but an historical actuality, as Hunter would have it, of the critic's position within the apparatus: her or his status ethic. Indeed, if we forget the critical interest integral to the theoretical bases of Hunter's analysis, we can see displayed the status ethic, not of a secularized Christian moralist wearing educational-critique clothing or an administrative intellectual of the bureaucratic state apparatus, but of a new figure, one belonging to a kind of post-professional middle class. The ethic of this figure is in the practice of suppleness, fluidity, contingency and the provisional. It is a figure urging acceptance of limits, even as its intellectual legitimation urges the opposing view that we work on our limits. This explicit "detachment from the moorings" of critique makes sense socially in the articulation of a new ethic for an era of postindustrial capitalism, or, if you prefer, postmodern governmentality.

While the detachment is "ethically" apposite, and fits a new constellation of self and social practices, it appears to linger in modernism long enough to want a moral stamp, albeit within its own autonomous sphere of administrative competence in the state. But, it is not easy to approve of administrative state virtues, living as we do in the shadow of the Holocaust and the Gulag. Franz Kafka warned about this administrative ethos: "Poets . . . are politically dangerous for the State because they want to change it. The State, and all its devoted servants, want only one thing, to persist" (quoted in Lowy, 1992:71).

The terror of the administrative state and its figures could be attributed to the moralists. However, we must acknowledge the historical actualities of totalitarianism in any apparently autonomous ethic that wants to remain only within the state's logic, by whatever name. This state, Kafka wrote,

> "has at its disposal a judicial hierarchy of high, indeed of the highest rank, with an indispensable and numerous retinue of servants, clerks, police, and other assistants, perhaps even hangmen, I do not shrink from that word. And the significance of this great organization, gentlemen? It consists in this, that innocent persons are accused of guilt, and senseless proceedings are put in motion against them." (quoted in Lowy, 1992:91)

This anxiety about defense of an autonomous administrative ethic—which I understand as a recuperation from the delusional hypocrisies of the secularized moralists, just as the rise of the state stems from the destructiveness of spiritual politics—may be needless. Perhaps the owl of Minerva really does spread her wings only at dusk and the administrative ethos of the state appears, in suitably postmodern flexibility, just as the state dissolves between the market and the spirit.

Commodification and resacralization, as I have argued, become the prevailing, polarized social practices. The deepest channel or most active site of this postmodern polarity is, however, the self. At one extreme, there is the commodification of self and relation; at the other, there is a series of cultural resacralization strategies that point away from traditional political charisma, to a transformation from within—a work on the self in sacred terms—that is subject at every point to profanation by incorporation in commodity forms, between new age religion-seeking and life-style engineering, occurring within a "liberation market." Simultaneously, as the new subject is problematized or constructed in this linked polarity, practices of desubjectification advance, following the directives of performance maximization that descend from the hybrid of rationalized entrepreneurialism.

What lies beyond this current dynamic polarity of social practices (while observed first at the self site) must be (after the long night) what Foucault called the "new forms of subjectivity."(1982) These initially are seen in a long list of particularist identities that on the global level appear as resurgent national and ethnic identities. Now, the terror appears as neither universal ideal nor administrative petrifying purposefulness, but as particularistic "zeal." The new forms of subjectivity—the work of the self on the self—can move through the moral universalist, identity particularist, and flexibly postmodern administrative solutions to a "new age" of social practice and understanding.

This new age builds on the core civilizations, submerged by modernism, in order to counter the deadening "mechanical petrification" by life-affirming practices. These practices are not morally induced, but are inductive artifacts of the self at work within the polarized apparatus. In Fromm's terms (1966) they are "experienced values." The counterforce presses social coding and dissemination of an amalgam of spiritual and scientific evolutionary knowledge and practice on the field of "arts of being" (Fromm, 1994). The creation of individuated practices necessarily draws cultural resources from outside the West European history of the last two centuries, within which all of Hunter's figures, heroines and villains alike, played their scenes.

I agree with Hunter that moral critique can be tiresome, but for different reasons. I see critique drawing us back, away from work on the horizon—work that has already engaged us with the "new" cultural resources of the ancients and all the richness that has always lain in the civilizations outside the modern West European ambit. In this work, a new language of social understanding can be built. As Michael Lowy puts it:

> Is it not time to break away from this positivist tradition and to draw upon a spiritual and cultural heritage that is broader, richer in meaning and closer to the very texture of social facts? Why not use the vast semantic field of religions, myths, literature, and even esoteric traditions to enrich the language of the social sciences? (1992:6)

And, in this work, a new form of subjectivity, a different way of being, is created.

From Postmodern to Resacralized

The continuing interest in social theory goes beyond the aesthetic toward the pragmatic and redemptive: the belief in social theory's effectivity, that theory is part of "the work" of self and social transformation. It is not the qualifying complexity and more sober realism of poststructuralism's revision of critical theory that I see as the historically revolutionary possibility. Rather, it is the collectively creative ingathering of the fragmentary, holy sparks from their current exile and dispersion. What that entails at every level, from the body that is not docile but enlivened, through a renormed, recultured structure or discipline of being, to the possibility of an institutional collective life that is vital and creative—is what we hope will be addressed as social theory takes its resacralizing turn.

Current social conditions, within which a strong dynamic polarity between commodification and resacralization work to delegitimate sociology and other modern discourses as uncertain wedges between a fully profaned instrumentalism and a tenuous questing toward sacred experience and religious language. New age social movements may new fodder for commercialized life-style engineering products or illusory compensations for the full success of the "mechanized petrification" of a rationalized European culture that Weber dreaded. Still, they open a gate to a very different cosmology of everyday life—a cosmology of an interpretive organization of experience and being on the other side of "economic rationalism."

The gate they open is toward the core civilizational cultures, particularly in their Gnostic forms (Merkur, 1993), which offer religious hermeneutics, or as Foucault had it, "ethics." What this means is an alternative to the secularized social cosmology of modern Enlightenment sociology and its antithetical—but joined—binaries in postmodernity, both in everyday life and in theorized sublimations. It is an historically conditioned, culturally inchoate, simultaneously individualized and commodified opening to new/ancient practices and discourses. It is dangerous and approached from a narrow ridge, fraught with all the destructive capacity of mystical escapes from the world: narcissistic onanism behind the pretense of various unions with the world; reimmersion in natural ecology; and, of course, the worst of all—organized social irrationalism. This final possiblity is too close a reminder of two words critical theorists, and postmodernists, dare not speak: the Holocaust.

This socially generated cultural unpeeling of modern secular social-explanatory cosmologies to reveal religious aspiration, experience and language only repeats Durkheim's explicit claim and Weber's scholarly practice that religion is the paradigmatic social phenomenon. Recall Durkheim's *Annee Sociologique* declaration that:

> it is these phenomena which are the germ from which all others—or at least almost all others—are derived. Religion contains in itself the very beginning, even if in an indistinct state, all the

> elements which in dissociating themselves from it, articulating themselves and combining with one another in a thousand ways, have given rise to the various manifestations of collective life. (1960:350, 351)

This sociological truth, the new age opening to resacralization, and the historical recency of the Holocaust, together, press me toward a particular religious hermeneutic. It is one that values the language from the archetypal margin, the difference within the difference that Singh (1995) identifies for "women of colour." It is a revivification of the redemptive calling of the Jews, the primal pariahs. This is not, historically, an entirely novel path as Lowy (1992) shows so well in his analysis of the intersection of libertarian utopianism and Jewish messianism between the world wars. Susan Handelman (1991) also traces this route in the works of Walter Benjamin, Franz Rosenzweig, and Emmanuel Levinas.

This is only a clue to a path that lies beyond critical theory and poststructuralism. It is a path toward Fromm's (1976) "city of being," and Levinas' (1994) infinity that is an alternative to the totalizing languages and philosophies of his renowned European teachers, who complied with the Holocaust. Before, beyond and outside West European culture lies the ethos of the East in the core religions and their dissenting aspect, which the turmoil of the present epoch unwittingly churns to the surface.

It is a renewal of this premodern core, in a postmodern historical context, that goes to prehumanism's original, creative redemptive revelation and its possibilities for a lived, interhuman being that we seek, as a way of life and as a language of social understanding. A truly new, transformative social theory and education are the practices of that social form.

Part Two

Resacralization

Chapter Four

From Social Theory to Religious Theory

The path through critical theory, postmodernism and new age culture, I have suggested, leads to a resacralization not only simultaneously within and against commodified popular culture, but also in academic social theory and in education.

In this chapter I want to explore this view more specifically: first, by showing how an expressly secular social theory of education can be read backward, to its unconscious origins in religious belief and practice. I take, for this example, one of the most systematic and well-known sociologies of education, that of the preeminent sociologist of education, Basil Bernstein. Second, I juxtapose this structuralist, orthodox reading, or revisionary "misreading," with the existentialist, heterodox, and ultimately mystical, but innerworldly, religious sociologies of Martin Buber and Erich Fromm. The template for this effort to follow social theory back to religious theory is, however, neither new age, existentialist nor mystical. Rather, I follow Emile Durkheim's hypothesis from *The Elementary Forms of the Religious Life*: "As we have progressed, we have established the fact that the fundamental categories of thought, and consequently of science, are of religious origin."

Religious Revision: An Example

Basil Bernstein's work is one of a very few systematic theories in sociology of education. Ironically, and, I think, unfortunately, recognition of this work has less to do with its explanatory efficacy than with its provision of a lineage of theory in a field of work characterized by a combined acultural and astructural individualist empiricism on the one side and an ideological, pseudopoliticized denial, in Bernstein's terms, of the "pedagogic voice" on the other. Bernstein's work, as a social theory of education, provides theoretical legitimacy to a field marked by division between not-so-Enlightenment social-science individualism and an historically frozen hyperbolic ideological collectivism that cares obsessively for power.

This use of theory as legitimation for other, non-theoretical purposes is not an unambiguous charge. For pedagogical discourse is itself, according to Bernstein, a "recontextualizing principle." (Bernstein, 1990) This means that recontextualization of Bernstein's work should not be judged too harshly, since the recontextualizing process is central in education and, more generally, in cultural systems and processes. Of course, it is not easy to be stoical about the inevitable recontextualization of one's own work (which is especially to be expected in the cultural sector of education, whose systemic work is recontextualizing meaning) when it appears as distortion, denial, or just plain ignorance and error. It is to Bernstein's credit that despite the disfiguring pulls to which cultural recontextualization has subjected his legitimating theoretical work, he remains able to stand back and theorize the criticism itself.

Bernstein's approach to criticism is not unambivalent. On the one hand, there is a sharp impatience with criticism as "a methodology of disposal; a field procedure for the displacement of theories of others" (1990:168). In the beginning of his *The Structuring of Pedagogic Discourse* (1990) which I take as a summative work, he complains that "there are few criteria which recontextualizers have to meet." While there is an acknowledgment that criticism may be useful, there is also concern about the "extent to which it obscures or recontextualizes the original text" (1990:8, 7). On the other hand, criticism is understood by Bernstein as a recontextualizing practice, and by his view of cultural work, it is a primary principle of movement in the field of discourses. Criticism is as necessary as recontextualization, but it is also a practice of avoidance and denial. Bernstein at once takes time to correct the errors of the critics and also to theorize criticism, as one would hope for a theorist of culture as recontextualization.

This reflective theorizing, occasioned by years of criticism of his own work, is incipient, with a major psychoanalytic theme, but with a minor note anchored in religious practice. Critics are engaged in displacement, disassociation, repression and projection. Simultaneously, the critics or recontextualizers may "sometimes perform priestly functions of exorcism, celebration, charismatic divination, and ritual succession" as well as other social functions. Recontextualizers can be recontextualized by their objects, as Bernstein displays. This human, relational mediation of texts is acknowledged, but it remains secondary for Bernstein to a more fundamental commitment to something that is less imaginary than creative replacement: the real text, the real intention of the author, and a real reading of the text that does not require either correction or reflective understanding of criticism. There are limits to recontextualization and theorizing criticism does not obviate the fact of interested error and misinterpretation in reading.

The psychoanalytic approach to criticism with which Bernstein begins this work has been carried further by Harold Bloom's revisionist theory of poetry (1973, 1975) and of culture (1982). Bloom takes the equivalent of Bernstein's "creative replacement" as the paradigmatic case of the cultural process. "Misreading" is not an error, but a creative "swerve" of poets fighting the "anxiety of influence" by their precursor fathers. In his earlier work, Bloom's view is that the culturally creative work of misprision, of "strong" misreadings, is the individually dynamic solution to the anxieties of influence and of mortality:

> Poetic influence—when it involves two strong, authentic poets—always proceeds by a misreading of the prior poet, an act of creative correction that is actually and necessarily a misinterpretation. This history of fruitful poetic influence, which is to say the main tradition of Western poetry since the Renaissance, is a history of anxiety and self-saving caricature, of distortion, of perverse, willful revisionism without which modern poetry as such could not exist. (Bloom, 1973:30)

In *A Map of Misreading*, he adds:

> To live, the poet must *misinterpret* [emphasis added] the father, by the crucial act of misprision, which is the re-writing of the father. . . . Every poem therefore has two makers: the precursor, and the ephebe's rejected mortality. (1980:19)

Poetry, criticism, reading and, in the later work, all culture, is an agonistic revision. Bloom goes beyond both psychoanalytic and literary critical understanding of revision as a defensive trope to religion, particularly to the joy of "Gnostic freedom" as the spark or "pneuma" for the "flickering presences, perpetually in flux" that compose meaning. Accepting "error" or misinterpretation not as mere defense, Bloom enlarges his earlier emphasis on the relational creation of meaning: "All interpretation depends upon the antithetical relation between meanings, and not on the supposed relation between a text and its meaning" (1975:76).

Education and Religion

In a discussion of symbolic control, Bernstein notes that Foucault's analysis of discourse seems abstracted from social relations. Then, interestingly, he observes:

> Further, Foucault ignores almost completely any systematic analysis of the common denominator of all discourses, education and the modalities of its transmission. For a theorist interested in normalization, produced by new discourses of power, to ignore education is one thing, but to ignore religious discourse is even stranger. Let us be quite clear: this lecture is in no sense an attempt to fill this gap, but perhaps to outline no more than a possibility. (1990:134)

Bernstein's own recontextualization of educational to religious discourse proceeds through a gentle and tentative misreading of Emile Durkheim. Reading Durkheim's *The Evolution of Educational Thought*, he asks politely about the distinction of medieval university curriculum between the Trivium and the Quadrivium (between time-bound communication and timeless explication): "Is it possible that the dislocation Trivium/Quadrivium is a metaphor for another signifier?" (1990:151). His condensed answer is that: "From this point of view the Trivium/Quadrivium dislocation is a metaphor for the deep grammar of Christianity and produced by it." What does the dislocation signify? "Thus the Quadrivium signifies the outer. The Trivium is about the inner, the discursive constitution of the inner. Trivium: inner-person-sacred; Quadrivium: outer-social-profane" (1990:151).

The "dislocation" that Bernstein emphasizes in his reading of Durkheim's account of educational history, I read as replicated in

Bernstein's own emphasis on dislocation which appears in his theory as an emphasis on "insulation." For me, the consistent underlining of insulation—of categories, communication, positions—is about not Christianity's deep grammar, but as Bernstein indicates, a dislocation, or differentiation, between the sacred and the profane. The insistent centrality of the principle of differentiating, the regulation of classification of categories of thought, as well as communications (framing) and positions (social relations), is a secular theoretical replacement of the principle of differentiating the sacred from the profane that Durkheim described as "the distinctive trait of religious thought" (1961:52).

I read Bernstein's fundamental commitment to differentiating insulation as a principle regulating difference in categories of thought, communication and social relation not as structuralist logic displaced to educational discourse or a Jurgen Habermas–type modernism of autonomous spheres defending against the recombinant degeneracies of postmodernism. In Bernstein's reading of Durkheim's educational study, it appears as reassertion of a religious principle represented forcefully in Durkheim's sociology of religion, reinserted into the domain of education.

The great emphasis that both Bernstein and Durkheim place on insulation or the creation of distance as a socially, religiously and educationally regulative principle resonates traditional Judaism's principle of "havdalah," or differentiation. In this reading, Bernstein recontextualizes Durkheim's sociology of religion to education, while Durkheim's description and claim that rites differentiating the sacred from the profane are the defining characteristic of all religion may be a particularly strong Jewish "misreading" of religion. To the extent that both these emphases on rules of demarcation resonate a deep grammar of Judaism, it is the rabbinic Judaism in which Durkheim was reared, the Jewishness of "the law" and its interpreted ritual application that gets represented.

Within, and often against, the Judaism of laws and rites there is a disfavored, if not repressed, tradition of a Judaism of consciousness, of a transcendental existentialism. If it is not Gnostic, then it at least contains what are usually called the mystical elements (Scholem, 1974; Buber, 1972). The resulting threefold "swerve" of this chapter, to use Bloom's term for the revisionary act, is from Bernstein's sociology of education to Judaism via Durkheim's sociology of religion, and then away from foundational, rational Judaism to the esoteric traditions of Jewish mysticism. Weber's Protestant interest in a consciousness of individual redemption is a sociological means for rejecting secularization of the rational/structuralist Judaism attributed to both Bernstein and Durkheim. Instead, I assert the historic Jewish commitment to practices of transformative consciousness and messianic redemption, individual as well as collective.

Differentiation ("Havdalah")

The degree of difference or demarcation is then the fundamental principle of social determination, as the regulator of classification in thought and practice. For Bernstein, "insulation" is the term for this determining degree of differentiation in classification:

> It is the strength of the insulation that creates a space in which a category can become specific. . . . The stronger the insulation between categories, the stronger the boundary between one category and another and the more defined the space that any category occupies and to which it is specialized. . . . Different degrees of insulation between categories create different principles of the relations between categories and so different principles of the social division of labor. (1990:23,24)

Insulation, the regulation of relational difference, is the primal social process: "Indeed, insulation is the means whereby the cultural is transformed into the natural, the contingent into the necessary, the past into the present, the present into the future" (1990:25).

Classification is the relation or structural foundation of Bernstein's theory of pedagogy and of social relations and culture. "The degree of insulation is the crucial feature of the classificatory principle" (1990:24).

The strength of insulation, or the degree of differentiation, operates in every domain—in classification, framing, positional relations, visible and invisible pedagogies, and the social division of labor, and as the equivalent of power. Insulation is not simply the regulator of categories of thought or discourse; it is the basis of society as well as culture. On the social division of labor, Bernstein states:

> Any position in a social division of labor is a function of the relations between positions. The relations between positions is given by the degree of insulation. The degree of insulation defines and regulates the degree of specialization (difference) of a position. . . . the principle of a social division of labour is the relations between its

> positions, or, more generally, its categories, and this relation is a function of the degree of insulation. (1990:99)

Insulation, as the regulative principle, parallels, I think, Durkheim's "interdicts," rules of keeping apart the orders of the sacred and the profane. According to Bernstein, education, as a social field or order of discourse, is reduced by reproduction theorists to "no more than a relay for power relations external to itself" (1990:166). Pedagogic discourse has its own voice, although Bernstein offers condensed analyses as well as asides identifying pedagogic discourse with a deeper grammar of religion and morality ("Briefly, all education is intrinsically a moral activity." [1990:66]) Metaphorically, the struggle to preserve pedagogy as being other than the effect of infrastructure may also include protection of what Bernstein describes as human knowledge from the impersonal market ("Knowledge, after nearly a thousand years, is divorced from inwardness and is literally dehumanized" [1990:155]).

This historical observation recalls Bernstein's differentiating ratios—inner-person-sacred; outer-social-profane—and the rules of insulation that create meaning by distance and differentiation. "What is to be preserved?" Bernstein asks. "The insulation between the categories," he replies (1990:23). Perhaps what is being preserved by asserting pedagogy's "own voice" against the "external" is the sacred and the principle of differentiation that shields it against profane mundaneity.

I read Bernstein's emphasis on differentiation through insulation as a "creative replacement," "misreading," or displacement of Durkheim's social analysis of religion to education. Durkheim's founding work is not a secularization of the centrality of the principle of differentiation. Rather, it asserts that the differentiation between sacred and profane is the subsuming center of religion:

> All known religious beliefs, whether simple or complex, present one common characteristic: they presuppose a classification of all the things, real and ideal, of which men think, into two classes or opposed groups, generally designated by two distinct terms which are translated well enough by the words profane and sacred. (1961:52)

Durkheim describes how the sacred is created and contained by practices of separation. "Before all are the interdictions of contact." (1961:341). The differentiation between sacred and profane occurs in practices regulating time and place in social life:

> In general, all acts characteristic of the ordinary life are forbidden while those of the religious life are taking place. . . . all temporal occupations are suspended while the great religious solemnities are taking place. . . . In the first place, the religious life and the profane life cannot exist in the same place. . . . Likewise, the religious life and the profane life cannot coexist in the same unit of time. (1961:345,346)

The need to create and contain the sacred/profane differentiation by a "negative cult" (1961:340) of insulating interdicts ("its interdicts are the religious interdicts par excellence") is expressed in relations between categories of thought, as well as in ritual practices:

> When we think of holy things, the idea of a profane object cannot enter the mind without encouraging grave resistance; something within us opposes itself to the installation. This is because the representation of a sacred thing does not tolerate neighbors. But this psychic antagonism and this mutual exclusion of ideas should naturally result in the exclusion of corresponding things. *If the ideas are not to coexist, the things must not touch each other or have any sort of relations. This is the very principle of the interdict.* [Emphasis added](1961:357,360)

It is this insistence of the centrality of differentiation by creating distance between the sacred and profane that I assert as the deeper referent for Bernstein's explanatory theory that relies so fundamentally and consistently on insulating classification of categories, communications, and positions. My hypothesis is that Durkheim's general theory of religion draws heavily and implicitly on Judaism's emphasis on "havdalah," and is not simply a reflection of his knowledge of aboriginal religion. Durkheim's analysis of religion, while unavoidably attending to individual "mental status," emphasizes ritual practices on the one side, and collective representations or categories of thought on the other. Both of these emphases, and their pivoting on interdicts of separating touch, sight, and concept in time and space, resonate particularly with rabbinic Judaism. It specifies as general religious characteristics a notably Jewish emphasis captured by the Hebrew refrain, "The Lord differentiates between the sacred and profane."

Max Weber, on the other hand, who shares both Durkheim's social analytic approach to religion and an awareness of the importance of the sacred/profane distinction, dwells on the subjective consequences of differentiating practices as a defining characteristic of religion. "The only way," Weber writes, "of distinguishing between 'religious' and 'profane' states is by referring to the extraordinary character of religious states" (1946:279). He underlines the *individual* religious state of being:

> that for the devout the sacred value, first and above all, has been a psychological state in the here and now. Primarily this state consists in the emotional attitude per se, which was directly called forth by the specifically religious (or magical) act, by methodical asceticism, or by contemplation. (1946:278)

For Durkheim, ritual practices, like the "par excellence" negative cult of interdiction between sacred and profane, "create and recreate" society. For Weber, the individual state of religious experience, while defining, is an insufficient condition for the religious claim to redemption. Religious states are sublimated in rationalized belief, which builds the sacred not as a recreation or preservation of social relations but, instead, as a call for transformative liberation. Dismissing the mere religious experience of his intellectual contemporaries, Weber wrote:

> A religious revival has never sprung from such a source. In the past, it was the work of the intellectuals to sublimate the possession of sacred values into a belief in "redemption." . . . Yet redemption attained a specific significance only where it expressed a systematic and rationalized "image of the world" and *represented a stand in the face of the world.* [emphasis added] (1946:280)

Weber's interest is not in the recreation of solidary social orders through practices and forms of thought based on differentiations that produce collective integration. Instead, religion is what offers the promise of standing "in the face of the world", not only as an individual experience, but as a rationalized redemptive call that effectively makes subjective claims which can lead to collective transformation. Not interdiction and recreation, but salvation and the varieties of prophecy are what gives religion its social interest. What Weber analyzes are the "different roads to salvation" (Weber, 1964). While the "religious mood" and the "personal call" are integral, the intellectual work of rationally articulating a socially transformative ethic was the most salient religious aspect for Weber:

> To the extent that a religious ethic organizes the world from a religious perspective into a systematic, rational order and a

> cosmos, its ethical tensions with the social institutions of the world are likely to become sharper and more principled. . . . Indeed, the very tensions which this religious ethic introduces into the human relationships toward the world becomes a strongly dynamic factor in social evolution. (1964:209-210)

I leave to others the challenge of "misreading" Weber's sociology of religion in relation to Protestant traditions, in the same way I have suggested Durkheim's as an extension of rabbinic Judaism and, of course, Bernstein's as a domain displacement of Durkheim's secularization of religion to education. My interest here is rather to turn the hypothesized foundational discourse of religion away from the analysis of interdicts, laws, rites, practices, and collective recreation—whether in religious or secular form—toward a contemporary understanding of subjective religious states and historically appropriate intellectual sublimations of these states that transform them into redemptive ethics for both the individual and society.

One step toward that goal is to turn from an exclusive analysis of a structuralist and reproductive Judaism and to begin unearthing an alternative, experiential and redemptive tradition, which in its turn, ultimately will be "secularized" to alternative concepts for social understanding. For social analysis, this represents a theoretical strategy of rethinking social understanding by reading or translating back past the categories of so-called classical, late nineteenth- and early twentieth-century sociology to the concepts and commitments of the historically core, religious cultures, from which, I suggest, sociologies are modern derivations. In that way, contemporary social analysis begins with greater cultural reflexivity or self-knowledge and makes a more conscious choice about the character of its primal foundations. The hope is that this "resacralization" (Thompson, 1990) of social theory, and attendant resecularization, enables a different and more historically efficacious set of social categories and practices.

Integration and Innerworldly Mysticism

Martin Buber certainly fits the pattern of an alternative to orthodoxy: an existential Romantic resonant with new age social theory. Erich Fromm follows directly a leftist Freudianism, through a humanistic Marxist analysis of "social character." One important commonality is that they both bridge secular and sacred solutions to the modern problem of alienation. They explicitly draw from traditions of Jewish thought and practice and so represent signposts for rethinking social analysis and overcoming alienation within contemporary movements toward revitalization through resacralization.

The trajectories of their work indicate quite different beginnings, but also a convergence of their later works. Buber is very much the Romantic, as Paul Mendes-Flohr (1989) has convincingly shown in his contextualization of Buber within German social thought. Buber's engagement with Friedrich Nietszche and Søren Kierkegaard is refracted in his mystical interest in "Oriental religion", particularly Taoism, and in "ecstaticism" more generally, but also obviously in Hasidism. Buber's path is one of socializing the Romantic, subjective individualist interest in "erlebnis," or experience, toward an ever more social, and ethical social, interest—first in his work on the interhuman, in dialogue, and then his emphasis on utopian community. Still, as Mendes-Flohr argues, Buber retains a core of German Romanticism, and, I would add, ecstatic religious interest: "Indeed, in that he continued to regard acts of the spirit, grounded in the realm of sensibility (kultur in the broadest sense), as the fulcrum of social change, Buber remained true to his intellectual origins as kulturphilosoph" (1989:126).

Fromm, on the other hand, represents a more recognizable (to sociologists, at least) Marxist interest in socialism and in the overcoming of alienation that he refers to as "dealienation." His path works through a "humanist" Marxism and revised psychoanalytic interest to social character and social change toward a new ethic of social being (1976).

Buber's overwhelming tendency is toward experience, ecstasy, and mystical revelation. Fromm's central direction is toward the grounding of socialist ethics in a more general and timeless "art of living" that works through Jewish ethical theorists, like Baruch Spinoza and Moses Maimonides. Yet, in his later work, Fromm relies increasingly on Christian mystics such as Meister Johannes Eckhart (1976), and urges that monotheism, from whence he derives his ethics of dealienated being, is ultimately nontheistic and mystical (1956:71). Buber comes to be critical of his own subjective individualism, as he seeks renewal ("incessant renewal") beyond the early work on Taoist unity and self affirmation in a "neue Gemeinschaft," a new society.

At first look, Buber's "way" (both Buber and Fromm come to the Taoist and Hebrew term, although "halacha" is very much a legal, ethical way) is, in Weber's term, an exemplary prophecy, while Fromm's more ethically based precepts for living represent the emissary prophetic mode. They represent the ecstatic and ethical types that were so central in Weber's sociology of religion and in his interest in claiming that the ethical, ascetic mode has been the basis of contemporary culture (the Protestant ethic). Weber, of course, astutely acknowledges that in cultural history, the types are mixed: "The most varied transitions and combinations are found between the polar opposites of 'exemplary' and 'emissary' prophecy. . . . in religious matters 'consistency' has been the exception and not the rule" (1946:291).

Still, the distinction, which appears to fit the central difference, within Judaism, of Buber's and Fromm's approaches to overcoming modern alienation—despite the convergence of Fromm's mystical interest and Buber's social commitment—is crucial to Weber as the palimpset for modern culture:

> Exemplary prophecy points out the path to salvation by exemplary living, usually by a contemplative and apathetic-ecstatic life. The emissary type of prophecy addresses its *demands* [emphasis added] to the world in the name of a God. Naturally these demands are ethical; and they are often of an active ascetic character. (1946:285)

Weber's famous thesis was the translation of ascetic, emissary Protestantism into the cultural foundation of modernity. His argument was based, in part, on the assumption that exemplary prophecy was, because of its lack of an unequivocal supramundane Lord of Creation, without an elective affinity for a practical, "workaday" ethic: "Wherever the sacred values and the redemptory means of a virtuoso religion bore a contemplative or orgiastic-ecstatic character, there has been no bridge between religion and the practical action of the workaday world." (Weber, 1946:289)

While Weber largely ignores the social-psychological consequences of the *innerworldy* mysticism, which, I suggest, is precisely the point of convergence between Buber and Fromm, he does acknowledge it as a logically possible combination:

> The contrast between asceticism and mysticism is also tempered if the contemplative mystic does not draw the conclusion that he should flee from the world, but, like the inner-worldly asceticist, remain in the orders of the world (inner-worldly mysticism). (1946:326)

This "inner-worldly mysticism" is not only, as I suggest, the common point between Buber and Fromm, but also is now culturally relevant beyond bibliographical Jewish interests. The social renewal that lies on the other side of postmodernism, that builds on a different site from the modernity grounded in innerworldly asceticism and draws from new age cultural resources ("ideational," in Sorokin's terminology) is initially driven by the dealienated experienced being of various efforts at innerworldly mysticism. If innerworldly asceticism was the religious foundation of the culture of modernity, and postmodernity was its decadent phase, then innerworldly mysticism may well be the religious foundation of the culture emerging beyond postmodernism. Buber and Fromm are potentially interesting when social analysis consciously bridges religion and "the workaday world" and defines its role as participatory in the practice of social transformation and renewal.

Buber

In reading Buber, here I will look at his interest in juxtaposing this emphasis on the sacred as one of integration rather than the differentiation of sacred and profane; in juxtaposition to Basil Bernstein's secularized and recontextualized sociology of education which is premised on the rules of differentiation.

In modern Judaism, Martin Buber clearly sets himself against what he sees as the dualism and rationalism of the historic Jewish mainstream. Not differentiation, but integration and unity are the hallmarks of Judaism, according to Buber (1972). Not religion, but religiosity—the state of experience, in William James's and Weber's terms—is what needs to be understood and lived. Against collective practices and interdicting laws and rites of differentiating structures and spheres of activity, Buber proposes "der Helige Weg," the "holy way" of unified existence. Unlike Durkheim, who sees a separation, or insulation, of the sacred and the profane as religion's defining aspect, Buber searches for integration and unity, by sanctifying everyday life, ending the dualism of sacred and profane. The Hebrew couplet that begins with "The Lord differentiates between the sacred and the profane," has the succeeding line "All our sins will be erased by Him." In other words, "havdalah" (differentiation) is a preface to salvation or for later redemption.

On this path, Buber carries forward to modernity a sociology of the "zwischenmenschliche"—the intersubjective, as S.N. Eisenstadt has translated it (Buber, 1992)—and of the utopian (Buber, 1963). His modern reading of Hasidism places this work within the long tradition of Jewish alternative movements that have been broadly referred to as "mystical." (See, for example, Scholem, 1974).

Buber's analyses and language fuse social understanding and religious partisanship, particularly in their critique of the Jewish mainstream: "I shall try to extricate the unique character of Jewish religiosity from the rubble with which rabbinism and rationalism have covered it" (1972:81).

What he wants to uncover is a religiosity of the Orient rather than of the West, a religion like that of Taoism and Buddhism, that offers "a way" or "path" aimed at a redeemed life for both the individual and the collective. Religiosity is not only an object of social study, but above all a lived experience, articulated in the deed as well as the word. The experience striven for, as in mysticism generally, is of unity, although Buber argues for a strong, particularly Jewish orientation to the attainment of unity:

> But wherever one opens the great document of Jewish antiquity . . . there will one find a sense and knowledge of disunion and duality—a striving for unity.
>
> A striving for unity: for unity within individual man; for unity between divisions of the nation, and between nations; for unity between mankind and every living thing; and for unity between God and the world. (1972:26,27)

Buber's emphasis on *unity* is as great as Durkheim's and Bernstein's on separation and insulation. "And it is stated with still greater emphasis: 'Only when you are undivided' (that is, when you have overcome your inner dualism by your decision) 'will you have a share in the Lord your God'" (1972:82). What he writes of as "the tendency to realize undivided life in the world of man, in the world of being with one another" (1972:126), aims to overcome the sacred/profane distinction. Buber was a critic of nationalistic Zionism as much as of rabbinism, although he sought a utopian possibility within the Zionist movement. In writing about ancient Judaism and its relation to Zionism, Buber underlines his ideal of overcoming the sacred/profane dualism and its boundaries by calling for a transformation of everyday life through an infusion of the sacred impulse to the profane:

> We must choose in this tradition the elements that constitute closeness to the soil, *hallowed worldliness,* [emphasis added] and ab-

> sorption of the Divine in nature; and reject in this tradition the elements that constitute remoteness from the soil, detached rationality, and nature's banishment from the presence of God. (1972:145)

Unity, hallowing the everyday, is the path, through individual consciousness and decision, to redemption of the individual, "the turning," and collective utopia:

> Unified, unifying, total man, free in God, is the goal of mankind's longing that is awakening at this hour
>
> All these principles can be summed up by the watchword: from within. . . . Everything is waiting to be hallowed by you. (Buber, 1972:170,146,212)

While Buber may be seen as the avatar of a mystical, utopian Judaism of unity and redemption, the so-called mystical tradition may offer more generally a dialectic that combines unity or integration with differentiation. Adin Steinsaltz (1992), in his contemporary "discourses on Chasidic thought," interprets Kabbalah to speak of the power of division, as well as unity. "Creation" is his textual basis for a kabbalistic dialectic of difference that begins with a "separation" or "sawing" of the first androgynous person into male and female:

> This tension between the two who had once been a unity corresponds to the entire system of Creation; spirit and matter, higher world and lower world, direct light and returning light, and so on. These opposites reflect the fact that even though a unified world undoubtedly has great advantages, it is rather static and perhaps even uninspiring in its inability to get beyond itself, whereas a divided world is much more dynamic and capable of change. . . . this breaking up or sawing apart of wholeness in order for something new to come into being. (1992:41-42)

These dynamics of unity and difference, of polarities, are of course central in other religious traditions, notably Taoism, Buddhism and Yoga. It is to these traditions that I believe we will ineluctably continue to turn as postmodern culture reveals no world-redeeming alternative to the European Enlightenment and its tributaries like "classical" sociological theory and its applications. Future "misreadings" will have to challenge also the religious discourses that I suggest are foundational to contemporary social understanding, as we strive to discover a cultural ethos that makes effective claims on subjectivity and intersubjectivity. To have also the "evolutionary" value that Weber hoped, to be collectively redemptive, such a culture will have to "stand in the face of" all the current orders, and in that sense, be not reproductive, but revolutionary.

Like Weber, and in this regard, like Durkheim, Buber overcomes alienation by proposing an ideal condition which he calls "the-between-people." In this state, transcendental energies, which originate in a direct, personal, creative religious encounter, flow over into intentional self and social regeneration through a social presence that simultaneously represents both mystical union and care for a personal other. It is a "living" humanism that combats what Buber sees as the inertness of both religion and society. Energy is created in encounter, in the "meeting." Here too, there is a sociology of presence and energy, which begins with religious experience, overcomes dead, or "I-it," social relations, to find and generate social and individual life energies: a path of renewal, regeneration and creativity.

Fromm

More than anyone else, Fromm made the affirmation of life an explicit foundation of his social theory. Nathan Gover (1984) calls him a "biophile." Unlike the classical sociologists and Reich, he openly derived a social theory of counteralienation through a close textual reinterpretation of religion. Fromm's (1966) "radical interpretation of the Old Testament and its tradition" sees the paradigmatic case of alienation as equivalent to death in the biblical struggle against idolatry. The key point about idolatry, for Fromm, is not the jealousy of a monotheistic god, but that idolatry, which he sees as "the main religious theme," (1966:37) represents death against life: "The idol is a *thing*, and it is not alive. God, on the contrary, is a *living God*" [emphasis added]. Fromm quotes Psalms 115: "They (idols) have hands, but do not feel; feet, but do not walk; and they do not make a sound in their throat. Those who make them are like them" (1966:38).

Alienation is a preface to its overcoming, which is signified by the concept of "the messianic time." In this time, writes Fromm,

> he returns to himself. He regains the harmony and innocence he had lost, and yet it is a new harmony and a new innocence. It is the harmony of a man completely aware of himself, capable of knowing right and wrong, good and evil. . . . In the process of

> history man gives birth to himself. . . . that man would become like god himself. (1966:97)

There is of course the crucial encounter with the divine, described in the paradox of the burning bush: "The bush symbolizes the paradox of all spiritual existence, that in contrast to material existence its energy does not diminish while it is being used" (1966:75).

In addition to eternal energy and the messianic time, which is the template for a "universal historical transformation which forms the central point of the prophetic messianic vision" (1966:109), it is the life principle and its affirmation that Fromm carries away from his Old Testament encounter; what he refers to as "the affirmative attitude toward life"(1966:141). This principle is worth quoting at greater length:

> Life is the highest norm for man; God is alive and man is alive; the fundamental choice for man is between growth and decay.
>
> One might ask how man can make a choice between life and death; man is either alive or dead, and there is no choice, except if one were to consider the possibility of suicide. But what the biblical text refers to is not life and death as biological facts but as principles and values. To be alive is to grow, develop, to respond; to be dead (even if one is alive biologically) means to stop growing, to fossilize, to become a thing. . . . to choose life is the necessary condition for love, freedom and truth. (1966:142)

Fromm's social solution is "to recognize this danger and to strive for conditions which will help bring man to life again" (1966:180). For him, that means a "renaissance of humanism that focuses on the reality of *experienced* [emphasis added] values rather than on the reality of concepts and words" (1966).

Experienced values have their origin in the realization of the "interpersonal fusion" that is "the most powerful striving in man" (Fromm, 1956:18) and the replacement of God as father with the principle of God. Ultimately, monotheism leads to mysticism, and theology disappears in favor of the experience of mystical union—a union that addresses the human need for transcendence and for overcoming the separation and aloneness of individual being. In terms of our discussion of Weber's struggle for freedom out of the iron cage by examining the cultural, and particularly religious "spheres," here too, there are ways out in both mystical union and love.

Fromm takes the interpersonal fusion of love not as an abstract concept, but as an "experienced value." That means love becomes a practice, an art, a virtue that can be described and actualized. Unlike Norman O. Brown's view, for Fromm narcissism is not the answer (the dialectic of narcissism is a crucial crossroads for transformative paths in the new age), but a sleep from which one needs to wake to the humility required for the practice of reason and objectivity. In *The Art Of Loving*, Fromm (1956) works through the steps of an existential practice that can overcome human separateness along the interpersonal path. The road is winding, but leads away from idolatry of self (narcissism) and other (masochism) toward a "rational vision" of faith grounded in courage and, ultimately, human "productiveness."

The practice of love shows how traditional humanistic values are justified experientially as a "path," an intentional right way of living, a Tao or Halacha. The practice creates life; by developing the elements of the capacity to love. The practice then "demands a state of intensity, awakeness, enhanced vitality" (1956:129). Fromm specifies what his solution means as a social practice—that people should "become as Gods," and so reverses Karl Marx's original model of belief in God as a human disempowerment. Ultimately, it is the capacity to love that recreates the energy of life.

Unless social and cultural circumstances prevail that make these rereadings real, they remain utopian, with at best an analytical interest in the study of culture, society and the individual as religiously, interpersonally and biologically driven energy systems that can, with right practice, revolutionize and transform the historical tendency toward their repressive alienation and death embodied in the current cultural order.

Like both Pitirim Sorokin and Mihaly Csikszentmihalyi, Fromm, in his later work (1976), describes movements toward a fundamental civilizational shift, an end of "the religion of progress," with its "radical hedonism" and "individual egoism," toward a "new ethic." Socialism is now expressly understood as a "secular messianism," a derivative of the Old Testament ethic of a socially organized, dealienated being. Like Csikszentmihalyi, Fromm returns not only to Hebrew humanism (to use Buber's term), but also to Meister Eckhart's Christian mysticism and the Buddhist Four Noble Truths as an ethical guide for the social psychological practices that constitute both an "art of living" and a "neue gemeinschaft," in Buber's words—or, as Fromm puts it, a "new science of man" to create a "new society." "If," writes Fromm, "the economic and political spheres of society are to be subordinated to human development, *the model of the new society must be determined by the requirements of the unalienated, being-oriented individual*" (1976:162). The "new synthesis" is "life-furthering" and in its "humanistic religiosity" aims to create a "city of being." Fromm saw elements of social renewal in contemporary revitalization movements: "I believe that quite a large number of groups and individuals are moving in the direction of being" (1976:63).

Renewal

Solutions to the modern, Marxist and Romantic problematic of "alienation" emerge now from within an incipient, but profound, cultural transformation. This transformation is occurring, without salient institutionalization, in myriad individual and collective practices, stereotypically grouped under the heading of "new age." Human sciences, including cognitive psychology and dissident social theory, have provided theoretical and empirical bases for the solution of the problem of alienation. They center on a social psychology of presence, attention, energy, or being. While sociology does not yet directly address the analytical implications of the noticeable cultural changes that are occurring, the cultural shift implies also a renewal of social analysis as well as of social practice.

The renewal of social analysis occurs by participation in the wider cultural process of "desecularization," as Fromm called it, or in other terms, "resacralization." With the assault on modernity, if not its supersession from within by postmodernism and from without by various reassertions of religiosity and spirituality, (social analysis' modern critical bridge role between religiously based core cultural traditions and commodified "workaday life"), there emerges a reassertion of the religious foundations of culture as both ethos and analysis. With a blurring of boundaries and genres well prepared by postmodernism, traditional ethical guides for living come to function more widely as systems of analytic social and psychological understanding. Sacred cosmologies replace the secular cosmologies that had replaced them, with the important additions of cumulative empirical scientific knowledge and new, more democratic, universal aspirations for self and social actualization.

Here I have described only some elements of this wider transformation in culture and in social understanding. What remains unfulfilled in practice in all the various accounts and premonitions are the organized, institutionalized social forms, particularly in education, which create and sustain the unalienated flow of transcending selves and a dialogical, streaming, resurrected state of being: Fromm's "city of being."

Sociologists have a particularly knowledgeable role to play in this social practice of renewal and reconstruction, but are likely to accomplish it only to the extent that we are able to surrender the decadent phase of modernity now called postmodernism and to accept the emergence and power of the culture of a new age and of the core sacred, civilizational cultures, repressed by modernity, which are now brought back to collective consciousness. Our task is to rationalize that consciousness, in the renewal both of social theory and transformative, educational practice.

Chapter Five

Revitalization: Religion, Society, Education

Opening

In the kabbalistic creation story, the holy sparks, which are the vital residue of an uncontainable supernal light, remain glowing in the dross of fragments of worldly vessels unable to contain them. So it is with attempts to reinterpret ancient traditions in contemporary fields of thought. We have some glimmering, but only within the prevailing cover of opaque and limiting fragments. What I hope for here is an opening toward those premodern traditions, and their inspirational "sparks."

For a social theorist of education professionally trained not in religion, but in American sociology, even an initial effort of this type of reinterpretation in the interest of social and educational revitalization is unavoidably clumsy and partial. Such an attempt is vulnerable to a forced mixing of genres and the appearance of religious partisanship. As to partisanship, I want to emphasize that I see the new age cultural opening directed toward all the core civilizational religions and especially toward their esoteric traditions: the mystical Protestantism of Meister Eckhart as well as the Islamic Sufi master Ibn Arabi; the Taoism of Lao-tzu as well as the Yoga sutras of Patanjali. Within Judaism, I do not consider the great medieval philosopher of reason and law, Moses Maimonides, less important than the mystical originator of the Lurianic Kabbalah, Isaac Luria—the lion or "Ari" of the medieval holy city, Safed.

My reading of esoteric Judaism, which draws on Franz Rosenzweig, Martin Buber, Gershom Scholem, Moshe Idel and Allen Afterman, is not a politically consistent one. Rosenzweig, for example, espoused orthodoxy and ritual, not mystical existentialism, while his utopian socialist colleague, Buber, is a salient target of attack for Scholem, the historian of Jewish mysticism. In turn, Idel and Afterman depart from Scholem in their interpretations of the multilineal traditions within Kabbalah, emphasizing neither Gnostic nor textual symbolic strands, but looking instead toward a particular frame of ecstatic experience and consciousness as the goals of theurgy and symbolic and literary practices. I draw on these often contradictory interpretations, favoring the experiential tendencies of Idel (1988) and Afterman (1992), beginning with Idel's distinction from Scholem's Gnostic interpretation of Kabbalah (and its generalization by that of his literary follower, Harold Bloom [1982; 1992]). For Idel "the Kabbalah is a genuine ancient tradition which is an esoteric interpretation of Judaism" (1988:32).

The esoteric interest may be only a bridge from Kabbalah to Halacha, the law, and toward more traditional forms of textualist interpretation or midrash. I recognize that these tendencies are interwoven rather than mutually exclusive practices and pathways. Further, I read from the outside, not as an adept, or as Idel puts it, one of the "perfectii," but as a secular social theorist with an interest in education as a socially transformative practice. In this sense, any such recontextualization, in Basil Bernstein's terms, is subject to all the limitations of cultural borrowing, despite some limited bonds and commonalities between the interpreting observer and the originating, native culture. My defense is in the promise of the heuristic value of this particular cultural borrowing for understanding society and education. I aim to encourage others who are content neither to rework modernity as "reflexive" and displace it into theory as "rational," nor to legitimate sociocultural stasis and decadence by an aestheticizing postmodernity.

Approaches

There are two complementary approaches in this chapter. First, in a global perspective, I borrow from several of the above sources in an attempt to move from new age sociocultural tendencies into an alternative language of social explanation. By focusing on the self in educational change, we not only move away from the superficial rationalization of the current performance-oriented, outcome-governed corporatism. Instead, I try to understand the directions of subjectivity within the historical, macrosociocultural changes that occur in the transition from postmodernism to resacralization. The self and energy focus of new age culture in what we have come to call "narcissism" (Lasch, 1978) is taken as a preface, search or opening for historical renewal at the individual, self or subjective level that I call "resubjectification."

The mélange of practices that seek, on self-centered grounds, to reenergize are understood as expressions of deeper processes of cultural change. The active element in those processes of change is the reinterpretation of the experienced reenergized subjectivity, a process that I call "resymbolization," in order to underline the *collective* symbolic or cultural work that occurs during such a change process. Resacralization is a process that combines both the energy concentration prepared on the stage of narcissism and the meaning or shared symbolic structure that frames and directs reenergized subjectivity.

The resacralization of social theory is a derivative, second order, rationalized phenomenon relative to the collective, more popular resacralization. The resacralized social theory that I bring to bear here in order to try to encompass and articulate these processes is drawn, especially and heterogeneously, from Scholem's historical readings of Kabbalah and Rosenzweig's descriptions of the cyclical ritual renewal of self and culture. These rituals alter linear, entropic and petrifying understandings of socially subjective time.

The second approach is at once more specific and more ambitious. Beyond very general notions of sociocultural movement in time, I try to descend from the macro-level outline of process to specify the interactive dynamics of relationality within larger images of cosmological creation and historical cycles. This approach is an extrapolation, drawing particularly from Scholem, Idel and Afterman. To the extent that the first approach addresses the macro-micro question, engaging resubjectification and resymbolization with creation myths and collective, cyclical ritual—self and cycles—this second approach indicates an analysis of social interaction derived from kabbalistic concepts of relation. While the movement of energy across worlds may seem farfetched to us, the conceptualizations in this cosmology ironically offer us clues for the specification of novel concepts with which to rethink social interaction and, correlatively, education.

Surprisingly, the relational concepts are, like our rereadings of classical sociology and the Romantic dissidents, replete with the images of energy flow and concentration, although, in kabbalistic sources, "light" is the favored term, coded often in terms jarring to us, such as "divine efflux," "cleaving," "boundless nothingness," and indeed, "holy sparks." While it is difficult for an outsider to capture the full force of this relational, interactive cosmology of energy, I do focus on several concepts and work to recontextualize and reconceptualize them toward a more secular, social theory of interaction that I believe will have implications for understanding and practicing education, as well as society.

The conceptual focus is once again on time, but less in its ritual cycles and more in its quality and with emphasis on irregularity and discontinuity. This is a way to begin to integrate and redirect our longstanding interests in social, cultural, and educational change, transformation and revolution. The sociology of presence, which I have juxtaposed as a phenomenon to alienation and as a theory to postmodernism's understandable preoccupation with absence, recurs here in what appears as a more metaphorical language, but is actually a much more grounded approach to "presence." Indeed, I argue that alienation theory, as Erich Fromm showed, is a scantily disguised representation of ancient Jewish descriptions and condemnations of idolatry. The esoteric traditions give new meaning both to alienation-cum-idolatry and to a sociology of presence by showing the opposite of alienation/idolatry in an energic, transparent presence, "light," infusing ecstatic adepts and ultimately, messianically, everyone. Individual and collective practices prepare and intensify receptivity to an energizing light that transforms the seeker, and then others and the wider community.

In this way, the self-other relation is rethought, so that individual development, so-called ascent, is necessarily integral to collective mobilization as both "uplift" and messianic redemption. These individual and social movements and their interrelation are no longer mechanical processes, but organic interchanges of light/energy, which are concentrated and disbursed, ebb and flow, pulsate as time, and are simultaneously self, other, and collectively transformative. "Presence" becomes not a static immanence but a dynamic potentiality, surpassing traditional social theoretic dichotomies of stability and change.

Presence is for interaction in this model what narcissism is to resubjectification in the macro self/cycle approach. It is a condition of the action for interaction that can be understood on the model of a transposition of interworld relations to this-worldly relation: innerworldly mysticism. Concretely, this means that, just as Fromm takes God as a model of man and overcoming alienation means "you shall be as gods," so the relation between God and his daughter's or bride's (in each case, feminine) presence in this world (her name is "Shekhinah") is a *model* for human social interaction. Still more precisely, just as the goal of human being can be seen as one of "cleaving," "communion," or "unification" with God's energetic, source-like, feminine presence, so the teleology of social interaction also becomes "unity" or "yichud," which refers to a series of bonding actions in which the prepared individual (ecstatic) state of development enables transparent unity with the other. Nor is the apparent sexual symbolism here a postmodern addition. Kabbalistic narratives, including the paradigmatic Song of Songs, are pervasively sexual, offering further difference from the innerworldly asceticism that provides the religious foundation for the culture of modernity.

From our sociological point of reading, presence becomes dynamic, merging with pulsating time, and the other relation of social interaction is ideally unified, becoming an effect and marker of self identity. "Becoming somebody" is no longer a defensive process. Here it represents repeated acts of self- surrender and intentional but unattached action, undertaken with equanimity, that foster individual ascent and collective ingathering and uplifting of the Shekhinah's exiled sparks. This process restores primordial integration of self, other, community, and world.

I explore then, in this second approach, the relation between Kabbalistic concepts of *time, presence* and *unification* and attempt to draw their implications for social interaction and energy, surpassing, as an ideal, alienation and its postmodern form of exiled idolatry in dispersion. The esoteric aim is the reparation or "tikkun" of the shattering creation of the fragmentary dross and the sparks of light and energy that they contain. Against the idolization of exile as dispersion, the messianic drive is toward the recollection of the holy sparks and their integration in a repaired, newly harmonized social world of reconfigured, fully humanly developed living beings.

Self and Cycles

The model of the dynamic context that frames my interpretation of self/educational processes is one that I am drawn to after a rejection of postmodernism as either analytics or ethics, and one that colleagues will identify as rejecting rather than reflexively preserving modernity, in favor of a premodern, if not ancient, understanding of individual and collective transformations. While I would like to think that this model only emerges as a convenient way to present the empirical observations, as I have indicated it grows out of a contemporary interpretation of ancient thought. At the same time, historically conditioned alterations in sociological discourse have led to what the American critic Harold Bloom (1992) calls "religious criticism."

Max Weber's understanding of modern culture as centrally a secularization of ascetic Protestantism is familiar and I have followed Arthur Vidich and Stanford Lyman who assert that "From the beginning, sociological thought in the United States had its roots in the Protestant religion"(1986:44). This transvaluation, transposition, translation or recontextualization (Bernstein, 1990) of religious to secular language—and further to secular cosmology or explanation as sociology—is, as I have argued, being *reversed* in the change in everyday culture that Robert Wuthnow (1992) terms the "rediscovery of the sacred" and Kenneth Thompson (1990) called simply "resacralization."

The implication of this religious turn, at least in the United States, for the resacralization of secular languages of social explanation has not been much explored, at least not by specialists in social interpretation. As I have indicated, I am aware of the incorporative, commodifying trends in this resacralization, as well as the cultic dangers of opening to that individually and collective irrational that engaged Emile Durkheim as well as Sigmund Freud and that Weber referred to as "the real kernel of social life." Yet, while it may be dissonant for specialists in social explanation to admit these discourses of the sacred not only as social facts or topics, but also as interpretive resources, it is precisely by understanding that latter possibility that an alternative model—and social and educational commitments—to both modernity and postmodernity becomes available to us.

Writings of the French philosopher Emmanuel Levinas have been described as representing a "movement from the dialectic to the dialogical" (Michael Smith, introduction, in Levinas, 1994). In the writings of Martin Buber, Franz Rosenzweig and Gershom Scholem there is already, underneath their significant differences, the sort of blending or even, in Clifford Geertz' term, "blurring of genres" between the religious, social interpretation and the individual and collective commitment and transformation that Michael Lowy (1992) called for. Further, there is a transformative model in their representations of both exoteric and esoteric Jewish traditions that, while it may bear more than a passing resemblance to dialectics, makes new social interpretations possible, and fruitfully maps recent historical self and educational processes.

This possibility involves an unorthodox interpretation of Creation as a way to understand contemporary self/education dynamics, an interest in Revelation as an insight to emergent self processes and educational changes and Redemption as a method for enlightening speculation on the future of self and education.

In *Becoming Somebody* (1992), I described the grounds for the realization of a class-differentiated process of social destruction, or emptying, at the subjective or self level. Simultaneously, the corporatist, instrumental and technical restructuring of school institutions that I have observed reinforces the subjective social emptying by a rationalization process that fits Weber's "universal rationalization of culture" in its pervasive, cultural emptying and desiccation. In a postmodern, postindustrial or corporatist form, this twofold absence of a vital social presence (subjectively and institutionally) represents the "mechanical petrification" or destruction as depicted in Weber's critique of industrial modernity.

This emptying and rationalization is the focus of critical theory's dialectic of Enlightenment—reduction to number, eclipse of reason, instrumentalization of thought, "amalgamation with advertising," and closing of society (Horkheimer and Adorno, 1972; Marcuse, 1964). From the vantage point of an esoteric Jewish theory of Creation, however, all this represents the first moment in a creative process. Indeed, the emptying and desiccation is not simply a "petrification." Rather, it is, in our terms, a process of cultural destruction, which in this theory of Creation, in this primordial, archetypal narrative-framing or model of change, represents not an end, but, as Adin Steinsaltz's (1992) and Scholem's (1974, 1971) commentaries on the Lurianic Kabbalah assert, a beginning. Indeed, the kabbalistic teaching is that the Creation is a destructive process.

In simple, contemporary terms, Creation is the result of an incapacity of vessels to contain the rays of light or energy of a chaotic world. The created world is, as Steinsaltz writes, "a shattered world that has to be corrected or reconstituted" (1992:7). According to Scholem, both this "breaking of the vessels" due to excessive energy, and the subsequent character of activity as restitution or harmonious recreation of the fragments—the repair or "tikkun"—is complemented by an emptying or reduction, a "tztimzum," of a divine center, so that there is emptiness for creation. Scholem's commentary is more complex and elaborated both in that there is an intended "cleansing" in the destructive process of creation, and that its purpose is not simply Creation but the grounding of evil in the world: "What really brought about the fracture of the vessels was the necessity of cleansing the elements of the Sefiroth by eliminating the Kelipot, [shells] in order to give a real existence and separate identity to the power of evil" (1974:267). Elsewhere, he acknowledges that there is a flowing of the light or energy and that an aim of Creation is "the restitution of the ideal order" (1974:268).

Scholem (1971) has strong differences with Buber, especially in the understanding of the history of Jewish mysticism, and Rosenzweig (in Glatzer, 1953) and Buber have different emphases on the Creation theme. My interest here is in the heuristic of a model of Creation as destruction, a model that entails a dispersed energy that sets the world task as its harmonious reintegration. This heuristic points us back to the historically specific emptying, fragmentation and rationalizing desiccation of the "school subject and class self."

There is a need not to accommodate rationalizing modernity, as Ulrich Beck argues (1992), but to see it, as postmodernism fetishizes and celebrates, as the positive destruction of an antecedent culture and historical subject. What becomes interesting, then, are not the reflexive accommodations, but the new forms of self, and their relation to education.

These emergent forms, understood as a process of *resubjectification*, appear within a variety of new age and religious movements. They also can be seen as a hollow self-centeredness that has long been the object of modernist critique. Following instead the ancient narrative, and its paradoxical substance, I want to suggest that the sequel to the current processes of emptying and rationalization is a resubjectification or reenergizing of the collective self (albeit coded as very separated, individualized selves) and that its medium or channel is our social-psychological object of critique: narcissism. If rationalization is the destructive agent of Creation, narcissism is the initial, recentering fulcrum of Revelation.

Revelation as Narcissism

In the kabbalistic grand narrative that I propose as an analogy or generic change model applied here to self and education, what remains of the shattered vessels, to be reclaimed and reconstituted, are holy sparks. The death of a modern Greco-Christian self, a self desiccated and petrified by the social apparatus of mechanized industrialism and fractured and fetishized in its dispersion by a postmodern ethos, is followed by a rekindling of those "sparks," which is in fact expressed as a contemporary focus on individual "energy."

The rekindling or reenergizing occurs on a social stage already set by individualism and by alienation. Their combined effect is to instigate narcissistic self-satisfaction as an antidote to powerlessness and the absence of meaning. The wave of social recuperation begins then at the individual subject level, with what Weber called "the transformation from within." And, the destruction of the antecedent societal waves has been so effective that the subject-level social renewal is consciously and explicitly directed toward shared, but individuated, practices that generate subjective energy. The narcissistic cultural frame does not merely serve consumption, but is a positive self-reference (Gendlin, 1987) that encourages a very wide range of practices that aim to rediscover, accumulate, condense, and manifest subjective energies—in esoteric terms, the shattered vessels' holy sparks.

Revelation appears historically as narcissism. Self-centeredness harbors the social labor of new energy production. Of course, the new energies can be quickly incorporated into existing structures and routines, as spiritualized commodities and reengineered selves. Resacralization is the societal process in which there is a reenergization of the self. Postmodernism is merely a preface to the mass resacralization of the self, which has evidently contradictory trajectories.

Resacralization of the self, despite its narcissism, becomes the lever for the emergence of a socially shared resymbolization that signifies a new, reintegrated social community and, thereby, Redemption. The self-resacralization, even in its individualized, commodified forms, finds a limit that presses toward intersubjectivity, and then toward retraditionalization. For "tradition," as Scholem writes, "is living creativity in the context of revelation" (1971:297).

This trajectory of Creation as destruction and of a social renewal through resubjectification—which, in its turn, leads to a new social community—is a path that Martin Buber articulated for the self, social relations and education (Mendes-Flohr, 1989): from a mystical self to a communitarian view of self and society. Buber's path illustrated how the focus on existential immediacy and the renewal of being can lead outward toward intersubjectivity and community. His early writings on education focus on personal unity and the overcoming of all dualism. Like new age education, there is an education of the spirit, for being, and of the body, for doing. Wisdom is unity through "embodiment." Even as Buber moves toward what Levinas will later emphasize as "the other," at the core there is the revelatory moment of the rebirth of being. Of education after a national liberation, Buber writes:

> The goal is greater than mere liberation. It is a regeneration of the very being, it is an inner renewal, a rescue from physical and spiritual deterioration, the turning of a fragmentary, contradictory existence to a whole and unified way of life; it is purification and redemption. (1963:157)

Later, Buber will write of a "longing for personal unity" that ultimately leads to an "education for community." The "rebirth of being" means accepted responsibility: the I-Thou, the dialogical relation, the movement from mysticism to dialogue (Mendes-Flohr, 1989). Buber sees this responsibility for the other, and the communion and community that it creates, arising out of the destruction of the immediate past and the centering on personal being in the present:

> In a formed age there is no truth, no autonomy of education, but only in an age which is losing form. Only in it, in the *disintegration* [emphasis added] of traditional bonds, in the spinning whirl of freedom, does personal responsibility arise. (1965:102)

And further: "But when all figures are shattered, when no figure is able any more to dominate and shape the present human material, what is there left to form?" (1965:102).

Buber wants to go beyond "the will to power" and "eros," which are concomitants of the quest for the renewal of being, to a self that exists only in between, in relation to the other, and in community. But this transition, from the revelatory moment of the subject's rediscovery of various forms of generative energy, requires more than narcissism. The transition begins with the very symbolic resources that make resacralization possible, whether consciously or not. In terms of our analogical cycle, this is the move from Revelation to Redemption. Empirically, both self and education are identifiable in the current new age, narcissistic revelation phase. But redemption of self and education in historical society is much less evident in any interpretive language.

Redemption as Revision

The redemptive process, seen socially, is the collective uncovering of the shared symbolic bases of self-resacralization. We see the most obvious deformations of this process in Jamestown and Waco, and in less violent cultic, fundamentalist collective conversion processes. We see it in decadent charisma and rigid traditionalism alike. The alternative is an active "conscientization" (Fromm, 1994) of the social unconscious. It not only adds responsibility for the other and community to a reenergized self, but also brings to common awareness the interpretive, cultural, symbolic bases of the energizing, individuated practices of new age movements. The restitution of the broken "vessels" is not only the embodiment of spirit and the vigorous unity of teaching and deed that Buber proclaimed as "hochmah" or wisdom. Rather it also requires the culture-producing cyclical rhythm of rites, as in Rosenzweig's understanding of Christianity and Judaism, and the articulation of meaning: a *resymbolization* that gives direction to the newly released energies of renewed being.

Energy, like light in the primordial kabbalistic grand narrative, requires direction and recontainment. As Gershom Scholem writes, in his commentary on Kabbalah: "It is a binding rule that whatever wishes to act or manifest itself requires *garbs and vessels* [emphasis added], for without them it would revert to infinity which has no differentiation and no stages" (1971:45). Scholem's commentary on Redemption stresses rejection of rationalist Judaism in favor of a messianic intrusion into history that is fully apocalyptic and utopian. The "renewal of the world," he writes, "is simply more than its restoration" (1971:14).

Still, messianic activism alone is insufficient for a new Jerusalem. The emptying of meaning in the apocalypse requires a complementary fulfillment in tradition. In historic Judaism, this means cultural creation within a tradition, but through its *revision* in interpretive commentary: "Revelation needs commentary" (Scholem, 1971:287). Tradition is creative and it is the "midrash," the interpretation, which effects intergenerational transmission and communication of the archetypal revelation at Mt. Sinai. The "pure being" of Revelation is not possible without meaning, which is the interpretation or resymbolization of tradition. "Not system but *commentary* is the legitimate form through which truth is approached" (1971:289). Put otherwise, "Every religious experience after revelation is a mediated one" (1971:292).

In the esoteric or mystical tradition, it is in the words themselves that light is found. Therefore, interpretation is the practice of an eternal present, since God's word is infinitely interpretable. "The ever-flowing fountain," in a sixteenth-century kabbalist text, "contains all diverse ways of interpretation." "The unending reflections" are the "uninterrupted voice" of a "constantly unfolding" creative receptivity of infinite interpretability (Scholem, 1971:300). Jewish mysticism, unlike textualism, is, however, more than interpretation and dialogue. Reminiscent of our dissent from Durkheim and Bernstein, it is an historically transcendent cataclysm that produces "a totality that knows nothing of such a division between inwardness and outwardness" (1971:17).

In education, the resymbolized self, which does not represent rigid tradition but rather recreates itself and a communal meaning, has not yet emerged. This resymbolized self is what our generic model of change hopefully suggests: a new self that moves beyond the current hegemony of education through self-destruction; diverse, but pervasive, "sparks" of resubjectification in popular cultural movements; self processes and small signs of the institutionalization of new age educational interests that we described in terms of body and soul. If, rediscovered, the generation of self energy is socialized and redirected, its narcissism can give way to creative revision of the traditions of meaning from which new age movements draw. This would mean a new renaissance. Beyond body and soul, education then becomes the vehicle of the revision of traditional meanings, by which a new culture is created.

I have tried to represent popular resacralization tendencies analytically, by drawing on traditions of ancient Jewish mysticism and more contemporary strands of Jewish existentialism. I take the cyclical model of Creation-Revelation-Redemption to be an analytic heuristic, offering a generic, if not primordial, model of change, but also a heuristic applicable as a frame of interpretation to empirically specific historical, sociocultural trends.

What I would underline for all of us interested in education and society is that if this scenario is at all correct, then the focus of education on self processes is perhaps the core element in wider current processes of societal change. Most of our attention is still rightly directed to present educational questions of class-self fragmentation and macrolevel rationalization processes. On the margins, we are beginning to pay attention to various new age and mass religious movements—and the implications of self and collective resacralization processes—as they occur within and alongside rationalization and commodification.

We may want to qualify our understandings of modernity and postmodernity and even to place questions of self and education within their problematics. My intent has been, on those topics, to look beyond the hegemonic and the marginal to a more distant horizon, both of the future and the past. Asserting the traditional basis of mystical revisionism, Scholem concluded his essay on revelation and tradition with this quote from Johann Wolfgang Goethe:

> "Das Wahre war schon langst gefunden
> Hat edle Geisterschaft verbunden,
> Das alte Wahre, fass es an."
>
> "The truth that long ago was found,
> Has all noble spirits bound,
> The ancient truth, take hold of it." (1971:303)

Social Interaction and Energy: A Kabbalistic Reading

The self-other relation, or social interaction, is not ideally an action of exchange or combination, or even of "meeting," as Buber would have had it. For the self is only an imagined crystallization, a substantial covering of inner sparks of light representing infinity that became separated and dispersed in the shattering drama of Creation. Their uplift and reparation is the latent force or drive of interaction, which insofar as it has a movement, is an instantaneously renewed moment of direction toward reaggregation, or ingathering, toward reunification and the wholeness of light or energy that is holographically present in every being.

In this paradigm of social interaction, time is understood differently, neither as monotonically linear "progress," nor as a religious foundation for secular Enlightenment that mistakenly appeals, as Scholem observes, to messianism for legitimation. Rather, time—subjective and social time—is seen as distance from infinitude. As Afterman interprets Adam's fall, it is a descent into profane time, "his awareness fell into finitude" (1992:35). The measure of life is subjectivized into a consciousness of the infinite and the whole. A "long life" is life lived with a certain quality of awareness, in recognition of infinity. Time as finitude (in our terms, alienated time) is separated, in that the outer fragments of this-worldly vessels, "the ten thousand things" of Taoist terminology (the objects of possession and containment) are worshipped or attached to. Idolatry of the fragmented externals of the world is both a reflection and extension of the exile of the holy sparks—Shehkinah's exile.

The immediacy of recognition of the infinite and eternal transcendental *holy sparks* concealed within persons is opposed to alienated time. This dialogue of the here and now with restoration and redemption is Buber's mystical existentialism, the "incessant renewal" of the lived concrete moment. It is also opposed to the alienated, entropic, deenergizing time of separation—the movement against exile—the *movement of return* from the living whole. The *movement of return* is the reintegrative aspect of time both as exile and dispersion. It is time that proceeds slowly in uplifting reparation or "tikkun" through intentional, but ego-detached, fulfillment of the "mitzvot," or commandments and laws that contain and direct diffuse and excess energy.

In Afterman's poetically condensed language, "the infinite is home" (1992:36). But, time moves neither only to the counteralienation of consciousness of the transcendental kernel of vital being, nor to the returning home where consciousness of the integrated and eternal is heightened by intended action and the collective rituals of temporal demarcation: the Sabbath, which is the preview of restored, harmonious, integral time; or the seasonal holidays, which more mundanely activate collective memory and ecological integrity. Time moves also across generations and worlds, in theurgies of cyclical and spiraling movements—rollings or revolutions of the wheel of individuated sparks and souls—and in theories of reincarnation that imagine forms of interaction before and after the body dies. Scholem describes time, in the kabbalistic interpretation, as the movement of the latent divine energy behind the "sefiroth" or potencies that organize every level, from body to psyche, relation, and cosmos: "It flows out and animates

Creation; but at the same time it remains deep inside. The secret *rhythm of its movement* [emphasis added] and pulse beat is the law of motion of all Creation" (1991:39). The same ebb and flow, wave-like pulsation "contains the ineffable that accompanies every expression, enters into it and withdraws from it" (1991:41).

This time, even in its most extramundane appearance, returns to this world, and the movement of interaction that is transcendental serves as an energizing moment of return to this-worldly social interaction. The drive for unification with the Shehkinah, or prophecies of celestial ascent to God's throne by chariot or ladder, are always complemented by stories of return to the social, intersubjective world. Return is the only safe path in the mystical quest for unity through cleaving or communion with the divine. Indeed, the cleaving or "devekut" is generative, not only the effect of ecstatic and meditative preparation, but also productive of new force, light and energy. Scholem writes about the socially interactive dynamics of energy: "This vital force, which is *aroused by communion*" [emphasis added] (1971:219). The person, according to Idel, is "viewed as a vessel collecting the divine efflux . . . a vessel receiving the Shehkinah" (1988:170). Mystical practices producing ecstasy are a prelude to unity or transcendental, divine bonding, which is itself a prelude to social interaction. As Idel writes,

> Furthermore, although devekut is a preeminently personal experience, it serves here as *an opening toward other-oriented action* [emphasis added]. Mystical union, or communion, thus serves as a vehicle used by the individual in order to better serve the community; personal perfection is transformed into a means of contributing to the welfare of others. (1988:53)

He continues, describing these mystical unitive states as "attempts undertaken by the perfectii to reestablish broken links between the divine and lower worlds by the mediation of their spiritual faculties" (1988:53).

Eternally experienced time overcomes the separation that is the condition of idolatry, or alienation. Indeed, Scholem argues that separation, isolation, or what we call alienation, is the very definition of evil:

> evil is nothing other than that which isolates and removes things from their unity, a process profoundly symbolized by Adam's relationship to the two trees in the Garden.

> The two trees are fundamentally one: they grow from a common root, in which masculine and feminine, the giving and receiving, the creative and reflective, are one. *Life and knowledge* [emphasis added] are not to be torn asunder from one another: they must be seen and realized in their unity. (1991:69-71)

Mystical union redefines the character of social interaction as a transcendentally mediated intersubjectivity. Just as alienation is deeper than the appropriation of labor power, intersubjectivity is interpreted as more than linguistically undistorted communication or empathy. Social interaction as intersubjectivity is mediated by a third, normally silent term between subjects. It is not circumscribed by the "between-people" or the "in-between people," in Buber's view of relationality. Rather, it is the silent but energized *presence*, the sparks or kernels of being within the shells of images and things, that is transformative, and indeed, finally, determinative of the interaction. The later mysticism of the Hasidim refers to the seeing of the soul's transparency, which is a transformative interaction. Another kabbalist view is that the silent space *more* than the interpersonal action is the locus of energy that mediates the subjects. For in that silent space is the in-dwelling presence of Shehkinah that is already there, in nature and cosmos, in all beings, pantheistically, and as systematic potentialities, emanations or "sefiroth."

Accessing this energic presence is especially the work of the perfectii, the pious ones, the "tzaddikim." Their "transparency," their becoming as glass (Afterman, 1992:12), detached from the congealing and concealing idols of self and object images, allows receptivity of the "white light," "electricity," or as Idel puts it, more classically, "the light of the supernal emanations" (1968:168). To recontextualize Bernstein's radio imagery, the relay is the clear pious one: the tzakkik, who draws down the Shekhinah, only then to mediate intersubjectivity and community by activating presence between the still spaces of mundane interaction and, in that way, revitalizes otherwise petrified and alienated social relations. Scholem writes of the Hasidic Master of the Good Name:

> the ideal figure is the man who fulfills the one central basic demand placed upon him: to live in constant communion with God (devekuth), so that even his active life will be filled with intention to raise the holy sparks that, according to the Lurianic Kabbalah, are scattered in all things and in all realms of being. (1991:127)

In Hasidism, an early modern revitalization movement influenced by the medieval kabbalists, the "tzaddik" or pious one takes on added importance and functions as an energy "relay" between the "shefa" or divine influx and a broader, this-worldly energy known as "hayyut" or, literally, vitality or life force. Scholem observes:

> The two notions—the influx flowing into the Tsaddik through his own communion with God, and the spiritual vitality always spoken here of his dynamic essence—become unified in a single concept of *vital energy* [emphasis added] flowing from the tsaddik to his contemporaries. (1991:130)

As if to underline the obvious connection to Freud's theory, Scholem cites the eighteenth century Hasidic master, the Maggid, who writes in 1770, "The Tsaddikim make God, if one may phrase it thus, their unconscious" (1991:139).

Further, our interest in "energy" and its relation both to libido and to kabbalistic and Hasidic theories of "hayyut," or vitality, is also noted by Scholem: "It should also be noted that the Hebrew term 'hayyuth' used by R. Benjamin and all of the early Hasidic writers to indicate the realm of life belonging to the sparks of a person's soul, corresponds precisely to what I have described above as the soul's field of energy" (1991:249).

Social interaction is revitalized by a movement outward, toward the supramundane. It is reenergized by glimpses of eternity and obliged by the task of reversing the exilic dispersion of energy that exists in the world as concealed potentialities:

> the "exile of the Shekhinah" has existed in the world—that is the separation and cutting off of the Shekhinah from its constant union with the upper forces that she was supposed to carry and transmit to Creation. It is now up to man to fulfill this lack. (Scholem, 1991:185)

Resacralizing Theory and Practice

Time, unity, and presence are conceptually resacralized here and, like the pulsating ebb and flow of reexperienced time, are also resecularized, in order to help make better sense of social interaction and education. One "descends to ascend," there is a back and forth. Like Susan Handelman's (1982) literary-theorist "slayers of Moses," we recontextualize or displace across sacred and secular domains.

"Displacement," she writes, "is both the *condition* of and the *answer* to exile" (1982:223). But our aim is erasure of that boundary, a unity of innerworldly mysticism that goes outside historical finitude to reenergize by communion with long-time potencies and then transforms quotidian social relations with its divine efflux—recapitulating and reintegrating the unitive, ecstatic state by revivifying and redirecting intersubjective and collective social relations.

It is certainly possible to try to overcome alienation and mechanical petrification by shifting to a more organic, vital language. This would be a language of light and energy; of clarity and communion; of apocalyptic breakages and eruptions into familiar historical time; of pulsation, unity, ascent, perfection, and surpassing of dichotomies for eternal, unified presence in a harmonious, integrated and radiant world. Yet, even this linguistic conceptual shift is insufficient and untrue to the character of the world view from which we are borrowing. It must be said, that the change in both language and concept can be at least refreshing against the stale shibboleths of current internal, abstract dialogues of European modernity. These dialogues oscillate between a glorious fetishism of artifactual worship of modernity's decay, in postmodernism, and efforts to resuscitate progressive rationality in communications, exchange and institutional reflexive models in modernist sociology. All the while, violent politics destroys the old lines and forms.

More is at stake than the refreshing novelty—as opposed to the routine, if not slogan-laden, academic critical discourses—in rethinking the cultural, religious foundations of social theory. The resacralization of social theory and education takes its cue from wider resacralizing processes, without, however, mirroring their conceptual content. My aim is to help create the opening for new and perhaps, ironically, more socioculturally appropriate models of social dynamics.

I am going to pursue this opening toward alternative models of social explanation that derive from an apparently "unscientific" world view. As I have suggested, contemporary cultural decadence and movements for renewal reopen submerged traditions, which then can be not only reexperienced, but also reinterpreted.

Both the experience and the interpretation are part of the theoretical revitalization process. Unlike the immediacy sought in new age culture, Scholem observes of religious, even mystical experience: "Every religious experience after revelation is a mediated one" (1971:292). On the other hand—representing the view that the revitalization of concepts is not a purely contemplative, intellectual, interpretive activity of textual commentary—Idel writes that "pneumatic experiences are viewed as a prelude to a particular kind of literary activity" (1988:243). In other words, for the kabbalists, biblical exegesis—Torah study—is the hermeneutic or textual aspect of a larger process of "embodiment" and the disciplined establishment of "altered states of consciousness" that *precede* textual interpretation. The "blending of action and contemplation," in Scholem's terms, is necessary for the simultaneous transformation of conceptual models and consciousness that is integral to sociocultural revitalization.

The cycle of ecstasy, union, interpretation and revelation is incomplete without the ingathering and uplifting of the holy sparks. The glimpse of eternity, even the exile itself, is an event or opportunity, in the infinitely renewable present moment of time, for uplifting, reparative action to recreate the unified light of the world. This mysticism is innerworldly not only in the way that it can be assimilated into secular social theory, but also in its obligation to transformative action and to education.

We have yet to "descend to ascend," to separate to reunify, to look at both the active and contemplative, the practice and the theory in education and social theory. We must pay attention to socially cyclical, subjectively and consciously plastic, pulsating time; to interpersonal force that is at once silent and wholly present and transformative of intersubjective dynamics by virtue of receptivity to silent presence; and to identity and unity, which may be hermeneutically achieved in community textual study, but which require individual preparation of altered states of consciousness, or intensified awareness. Attending to all this only opens the gate for a radical alterity, for that which is entirely other.

This departure from the underlying religiocultural assumptions (which form the base of the social theories and educational practices that we wish to supersede and that various contemporary cultural movements challenge) strives to break their presumptive spell, their taken-for-granted "naturalness," and has only been initiated here. Like the resacralization of culture itself, the resacralization of theory and the conscious transformative practice of education is a community-based, collective task. We hope to stimulate some energy for that task and to encourage receptivity to the social, secular rethinking of ancient religious traditions as a resource for contemporary social understanding.

Chapter Six

Resacralizing Education

Education and Sociocultural Change

Like analytic social languages, educational practice also changes with sociocultural evolution. We ordinarily start with the modern era and observe the institutional establishment of schooling with the rise of industrialism and, concomitantly, its routinization along with the organization of educational bureaucracies. As we have seen, recent works such as Ian Hunter's (1994) recognize the religious prehistory of schooling and its transmutation into a governmental apparatus of pastoral bureaucracy. In such a formation, the creative potentials of self-transformation and resacralization are displaced and simultaneously split into performing the postindustrial moral discipline of the school—"the vocational ethic taught by an ascetism that is oriented to the control of the terrestrial world—and the "flight into the irrationalities of apolitical emotionalism" (Weber, 1963:236). The "increased tendency" of "apolitical emotionalism" is "one of the actual consequences of the rationalization of coercion", as pastorally exercised by schools and becoming epidemic as the national state becomes the postmodern corporatist global village (Weber, 1963:236). What postmodernism as a social form will mean for schooling is not yet adequately documented, although those of us actively engaged in contemporary movements for the social reform of educational practice have some less systematic, but direct observations of the direction and meaning of these changes.

With each alteration of institutional direction and sociocultural premise, definitions and practices of teaching and learning also have shifted, though lagging behind other social sectors—notably the economic—and so giving fuel for the work of educational reformers. The rise of the factory school and its reorganization in terms of industrial efficiency has been described in detail (Callahan, 1962). My earlier description of educational corporatism indicates contemporary signs of "breaking the mold" of that factory school in favor of a corporate, flexibly postmodern "Toyota" school.

Along with, but still marginally connected to, this main corporate tendency are small ripples emanating out of the new age culture's educational expression. One can see these ripples in the exploration of body education and even in smaller instances of education for awareness, meditation, or, in Buddhist terms, "mindfulness." A larger ripple that can be felt from the emergent margins is of a cultural reorientation that this movement defines as a moral and ethical renewal in community building and, as an educational corollary, character education. In the United States, a "communitarian network," led by the sociologist Amitai Etzioni and others, has now held two annual "White House conferences" (Demott, 1994) in an effort to mobilize national educational policy support for a morally restorative, consensual, communitarian definition of character education.

The corporatist, postmodern tendency is neither the postmodernism of aesthetic pastiche, nor postmodernism as a resuscitated demand for renovated liberal pluralism. Rather, postmodernism in education is fiercely postindustrial. It is a reform movement that is scrambling to meet the demands of corporately restructured businesses, which in turn are responding to massive changes in technology and the marketplace. This change led by corporate business corresponds to the earlier efficiency movement in education that Callahan (1962) described not as a conspiratorial business imposition, but rather as a response from educators to meet the clear expectations of the most powerful and vocal actors in the public domain: business leadership. Now that corporate measures for restructuring are at least justified, if not caused, by intensified global competition and the electronic communications revolution, these same measures are increasingly transported across institutional sectors as social and organizational solutions for education and, thereby, for society (Noble, 1996; Mickelson, 1996).

The business and governmental press for new skills as embodied in the national education agenda called America 2000 refers not only to computerization and information, but also to the social organization of teaching and learning. Increasingly, social and economic investment in schooling must be defended against charges of economic inefficiency and unproductivity (Hanushek, 1994). What follows from that is the institutionalization of devices of regulation that offer postmodern examples of what Michel Foucault's (1977) oeuvre describes for the emergence of industrial-style governmentality. This institutionalization posits the biopower of early social science and Enlightenment languages as panoptic surveillance. Now not social science, but corporate terms and mechanisms of organization and production increasingly serve to reorder the practices of teaching and students' experiences of learning.

While industrial education always was characterized by measurement, its character was more bureaucratic than corporate. Appropriately for postmodernism, new measurement is flexible and polyvocal, even authentic, in its retreat from the sublimation of performance into tests as literary abstracted devices. Instead, industrial education changes its locus of measurement from test to performance, and its calibration of the measurement of real-life skills as those qualities actually required by new work tasks. Evaluation is bound to accountability. Rewards for educational performance are recoded from educational into corporate languages of productivity. The measurement and evaluation focus, albeit flexible, is in fact increasingly aimed toward the national homogenization of school curricula and student learning standards. Finally, this focus of evaluation extents to the voluntary self-testing of teachers according to individualized ("customized," in postindustrial terms) outcome-based standards of professionalized restratification of the labor force of teachers. The corporatist, as opposed to the merely corporate, aspect of this social rationalization of performance-measured restratification of students and teachers is the extent to which a plethora of standards projects are regulated by combined elites from business, government and educational sectors, including representation by teachers and teacher-union leaders.

Against this overwhelming social movement for the institutionalization of postindustrial, or postmodern practices and languages in education, there is virtually no opposition. Character-education advocates may assert that morals and ethics are needed to insure education that sustains the national social fabric, without challenging the postindustrial reorganization of schooling. A few marginalized, alternative schools may teach their students relaxation and breathing techniques, or perhaps even yoga positions. But the mass, mainstream educational interest plays catch-up to models of corporate restructuring and laments insufficient levels and measures of student performance.

Socioeducational Criticism

During this time of great socioeducational turmoil, critical and postmodern sociologists as well as social theorists of education offered as criticism only a tired repackaging of increasingly mechanical images and orientations to politicize education through "critical pedagogy." The starting point in the recent history of social interpretation in education is ideology-critique, as part of a cultural movement that I think we may now call the cultural revolution of the sixties. In this movement of mass and academic culture, social institutions and discourses were debunked as impostors of objectivity and neutrality, in favor of political, socially interested critiques of power and its falsely neutralized, legitimating representations (Gouldner, 1970; Blackburn, 1972).

This movement dashed sociological functionalism, with its social-functions-of-the-classroom analyses of teaching and learning (Parsons, 1961; Dreeben, 1968) and its view of education as a process of socialization to shared social values and appropriate, role-prescribed behaviors. The new sociology brought class conflict and domination into the school and to a wider social-analytical shift in which society substituted conflict for integration and an antinomy of reproduction and resistance in education for any smoothly internalized acquisition of the status quo by an ordered division of labor that predicted unproblematic socializing identification as central in the educational process (Parsons, 1955).

The sparkling patina of this sociology of education shone from England to North America and enabled an occasional dissolving of borders between curriculum and sociology (Wexler, 1987). This border dissolve was reflected most popularly in the work of Michael Apple (1979;1982) and Henry Giroux (1983). This work continues in contemporary applications to postmodernism and feminism and in uses of later continental theories of difference and domination for purposes of social educational critique (Aronowitz and Giroux, 1991; Apple, 1993).

The obvious implication for teaching has been the effort to work from social criticism to an alternative educational practice that would embody this criticism, a view best captured by the term "critical pedagogy." Of this implication, Peter McLaren writes:

> At the same time, many current trends in critical pedagogy are embedded in the endemic weaknesses of a theoretical project overly concerned with developing a language of critique. Critical pedagogy is steeped in a posture of moral indignation toward the injustices reproduced in American public schools. (1995:32)

Jay and Graff (1993) excoriate critical or radical pedagogy more directly—and more saliently to the question of teaching:

> What worries us is the way that efforts by teachers to empower students often end up reinforcing the inequalities of the classroom. This is clearest when teachers directly promote progressive doctrines in their courses, merely inverting the traditional practice of *handing* knowledge *down* to passive students who dutifully copy it into their notebooks. (1993:1, 15)

Of the guru of critical pedagogy, Paulo Freire, they write:

> In picturing the classroom, Freire and other proponents of critical pedagogy seemingly envisage a teacher who is already committed to social transformation and simply lacks the lesson plan for translating the commitment into practice.
>
> It means that critical pedagogy is usually a business of preaching to the converted, leaving the unpersuaded overlooked, alienated, and receptive to the counter propaganda of conservatives. (1993:1,15)

In a poststructuralist reading of critical educational theory, Jennifer Gore notes:

> A cynical reading might suggest that such a trajectory attempts to dignify educational theorizing within the academy rather than teachers' work for itself. . . . We might ask whether the notion of teacher as "transformative intellectual" functions in the interests of students, teachers, "social change" and/or the theorist. While Giroux (1988) argues strongly that this notion is beneficial to teachers, students and the whole project of educational and social change through critical pedagogy, the fact that it does not seem to have been widely embraced by either teachers or other

> educational theorists suggests that its resonance with others in the educational community has been limited—or that few have heard of it. (1993:101,102,103)

She continues her critique of critical pedagogy:

> As further evidence of critical pedagogy's universalizing or totalizing tendencies, consider again the language that asks teachers to "engage unyieldingly in their attempts to empower. . . ." Such words connote not only a refusal to compromise but also a certainty about the "proper" approach that leaves little space for tentativeness or openness. (1990:102)

Complementary to critical pedagogy, the new sociology encouraged a wave of what Gary Anderson (1989) called "critical ethnography" in education. Against the variable analysis that defined the prerevolutionary movement of the 1960s and continues to characterize the mainstream of American sociology of education, there was an enormous wave of work that tried to achieve some methodological concretion, particularity in socially critical descriptions of school life. Understood as a social and cultural phenomenon itself, this critical ethnography may have represented still another incipient and incorporated attempt to overcome more general alienation and to develop a record of social-science research performance. And, like broader individuated and collective strategies of escape from alienation, domination and inequality, it was drawn back into a powerful hegemony of an administrative and consumptionist logic that pervades schooling (Hunter, 1994; Wexler, 1987) no less than research or everyday social life.

The new sociology of education was part of the larger academic and cultural revolt against inequalities and alienation in the administered, culturally complacent society. The postmodernism that followed it offered new languages and fuel for cultural criticism (Smith and Wexler, 1995). But in education, and perhaps more broadly, it did not stem the individual and institutional effects of deepening inequality, administrative rationalization, and self-alienation. Behind the critical front of postmodern discourse, a pervasive process of social emptying took place in social educational life.

Within the overarching cultural change, the educational tendencies are contradictory. Narcissism and body education, with their dialectic of emancipatory though unsocialized possibilities, are accompanied by further and deeper organic petrification and corporatist commodification. The implications of body and, indeed, soul education remain largely at the theoretical and research level, with the exception of more traditional Gnosticism, which may be appropriated by rethinking isolated educational instances, such as movements like Steiner schools. The main educational tendency, at least in the United States, remains the corporatist, productionist emphasis, in the public sector and in the restructuring of schools. The third possibility that I indicated is what now emerges as a need for a remoralized corporatism, a communitarian-style character or values education. Yet this possibility is still offered as ancillary, rather than as an alternative, to the cultural neglect of the corporatist restructuring of education.

The practical, educational effects of the broader cultural transformation that I am indicating, one well outside and beyond the emergent liberal binary of the economistic (corporatist) and culturalist (character education) programs, are institutionalized only in the most fragmentary forms. Both the economic and cultural liberal interests are forging educational change by a successful mobilization of broad-scale networks, while new age culture has been most successfully networked only in its commodified, commercial forms. Its transformative aspect remains local, body-centered and eclectic in the reintellectualization that can provide a necessary groundwork for legitimation and mobilization. This educational movement, which will provide a real alternative to the hegemonic binary of education either for postindustrial work or moral character, remains diffuse and uncrystallized at the larger network levels, where the collective mobilization required to change mass institutional practice can be accomplished.

Toward Resacralized Teaching

The complex series of ambivalent cultural movements that I have called new age do make it possible to imagine a more deeply alternative approach to teaching, one that pits itself directly against the instrumentalizing rationalization of current pedagogic emphases on performance for the Toyota school. Of course, the current religious turn in culture can have the same incorporative result as commodified new ageism and authoritarian critical pedagogy (a left authoritarianism that is a modern version of the "will to power" that Buber wished to avoid in education). What makes the deeper alternative now culturally possible, however, is a conjuncture of interest in energy, religion and everyday social interaction.

In the first instance, teaching is, to use Mihaly Csikszentmihalyi's (1993) application of the interest in energy to cognitive psychology, the opposite of entropy or energy loss. It is "negentropy:"

> But entropy is not the only law operating in the world. There are also processes that move in the opposite direction: creation and growth are just as much part of the story as decay and death. Beautifully ordered crystals take shape, new life-forms develop, increasingly improbable methods of exploiting energy emerge. Whenever order in a system increases instead of breaking down we may say that negentropy is at work. (1993:20)

Buber says the same, in the language of existentialism:

> In every hour the human race begins. We forget this too easily in the face of the massive fact of past life, of so-called world history. . . . *in spite of everything* [emphasis added], in this as in every hour, what has not been invades the structure of what is . . . a creative event if ever there was one, newness rising up, primal potential might. This potentiality, streaming unconquered, however much of it is squandered, is the reality *child:* this phenomenon of uniqueness, which is more than just begetting and birth, this grace of beginning again and ever again. (1965:83)

The desire for negative entropy that is so evident in new age culture leads, as I have suggested, at first to narcissism. But narcissism is insufficient to the task of resubjectification. It moves outward, to the environment, to whole energy—to "have" (Fromm, 1976) and to grasp. Our environment increasingly responds virtually, with the condensed consumption of the automatic images of television and personal computer screens. This voyeurism is like narcissism, like environmental dependency and addiction, in its greed for energy by having to have the image of the other, to possess the image of the object. Both the narcissism of commodified new age fetishism and the voyeurism of imaginary, virtual, information culture create a gap between interaction and relationality. This narcissism and fetishism deprive rather than nourish the microsocial interactional conditions of teaching and learning as creativity and growth and negate resubjectification and resymbolization which lead to teaching as redemption.

Under these sociopsychocultural conditions, what makes redemptive teaching possible? My view is that the cultural trajectory that I have outlined, and which is now in a mass resacralization of self and culture, sets the stage for teaching as negentropy and as the kind of historically redemptive interaction or relational intersubjectivity that Martin Buber (1992) envisioned. This becomes culturally and interactionally possible to the extent that the religious turn in contemporary culture, especially the renewal of esoteric traditions in all the classical world religions (Merkur, 1993), functions collectively as well as individually in a useful cultural regression.

The term "regression" follows the psychoanalytic understanding with the qualification of "regression in the service of the ego," which indicates a developmentally healthy and, indeed, creative regression. (See also Stephen Appel's application [1992] of psychoanalysis to sociology of education). Kevin Fauteux (1994) describes the traditional psychoanalytic view with Ernest Kris's revision of an adaptive value for regression, particularly as seen in the creative process of artists. What Fauteux adds is an understanding of religious experience, following Sigmund Freud, as emotionally and symbolically regressive. However, in Fauteux's view, religious experience (following William James) can provide the same adaptive regression as art or other individual forms of ego regression.

The interpretation of the regressive process as one that enables expression and experience of the sense of communion that gets suppressed in the individuating path of autonomous ego development is especially relevant for a cultural, historical or contextual social understanding of teaching. Such a trusting communion, seen in the light of a positive view of regression, has the effect of fostering creative insight and growth. When the regressive experience is reassimilated to the ego, it enables symbolic elaboration, which is a communication, or teaching, of the reexperienced trust, communion and receptivities of unitive experience.

This, of course, is the best of art and mysticism. It is elaborative, expressive, and posits a return to the world of others. Fauteux observes: "Religious experience restores the communion structures that existed prior to the anxious development of a separate self and hence prior to the fears, conflicts, and basic fault that formed out of the infant's earliest unitive state" (1994:154). Fauteux is making two important points. First, a psychological process of regression must be understood in its adaptive, elaborative, and creative aspect. Second, religious experience is one channel or medium of this creative regressive psychological state. In a sense, religion may function as "a transference" for primary object relations, and regressively restore the basic trust and communion of interactional unity, in a symbolic mode.

From the vantage point of our cultural and pedagogic interest, there are a number of implications in such a model. As Weber (1946) hoped, religion, replete with all the dangers that he perceived as strongly as Freud did, can be an antidote to the mechanical petrification and death of the industrial, administrative apparatus; however, it actually may have become the unintended heir of a similiar death: ascetic historical religious tendency. The unitive emphasis helps explain the particular contemporary appeal of the esoteric and mystical-spiritual interests in the lives of the baby boomers whom Wade Roof (1993) studied.

This circuitous cultural path, through what I am calling "the religious transference," reopens an intersubjectivity that has been socially emptied in the institutional rationalization process managed by class-differentiated, defensive selves. The religious transference facilitates trust and, therefore, social interaction or intersubjectivity. In a view of teaching that is not limited to skill transmission, but rather aims at growth, transformation and creativity, these are the first cultural, then interactional, conditions of possibility. What the religious transference does (since, as we have argued, the religious turn is part of a mass cultural, as well as theoretic, reversal) is to create these conditions for creative regression. It does this by a symbolic transference of religion as an individuated, but widely shared, *collective process.*

Resacralized, redemptive teaching then does not mean teaching religion. What it does mean is that cultural conditions exist that facilitate the sort of intersubjectivity, relationality or, simply, social interaction that is simultaneously part of a collective process of sociocultural renewal (resymbolization) and part of individual transformation and development (resubjectification) that we understand as constituting education. These interactional, relational possibilities are described also in Jessica Benjamin's (1988) critical feminist psychoanalytic approach to domination and to its opposite, which she terms "mutual recognition":

> What I call *mutual recognition* includes a number of experiences commonly described in the research on mother-infant interaction: emotional attunement, mutual influence, affective mutuality, sharing states of mind. The idea of mutual recognition seems to me an ever more crucial category of early experience. (1988:16)

Benjamin underlines the duality of interaction between assertion and recognition and argues that contemporary culture overemphasizes assertion and individuation at the cost of sacrificing communion, so that: "The image of the other that predominates in Western thought is not that of a vitally real presence but a cognitively perceived object" (1988:78).

Intersubjective mutuality is negentropy and supplants narcissism and voyeurism as the prevailing form of social interaction. Redemptive teaching is the strong form of this mode of interaction. In Buber's formulation, there is an "experience of inclusion of the other side" (1965:97). In teaching, there is "that subterranean dialogic, that steady potential presence of the one to the other is established and endures. Then there is reality *between* them, there is mutuality" (1965:98). Buber's pedagogic language foreshadows contemporary feminist psychoanalytic and humanist relational models in his understandings of trust, communion and communication ("The relation in education is one of pure dialogue").

Interest in the sociocultural context of teaching and learning represents an attempt to avoid pedagogic idealism. I offer Buber's dialogic model as an example, not simply as a goal of teaching, but as an interactional possibility, brought to the fore by changed social and cultural conditions. Whether such examples are transhistorical ideals, I do not know. But, I do think that our ability to reach toward such an ideal now is the effect of our current location in the recent trajectory of sociocultural evolution.

What such an ideal suggests is that it is the vital presence of the teacher, who concentrates the social world and its possibilities in his or her presence and is more important to the process of education than skill training in assessment or organizational effectiveness, that needs to be addressed. This would mean an entirely different repertoire for teacher education, an education of teachers for being and meaning and for the capacity to creatively include the student and the possibilities of other social world(s) and times.

And, in Harold Bloom's kabbalistic reading of literary criticism, his use of the term "hyperbole" as a trope may also characterize this wider cultural, historical process that now contextualizes teaching: "where something emptied out is heightened again to fullness" (1975:78).

Teaching as Being

Buber's dialogical interaction—and particularly dialogical teaching—works from the starting point of "presence." Here, Buber does not ordinarily mean the in-dwelling spiritual presence that we have described kabbalistically as Shekhinah. Education, for Buber, is openness toward what he calls "the creative Spirit." Presence is existential, concrete, mutual and inclusive of the other in a way that goes beyond psychological empathy. "Inclusion is the extension of one's own concreteness, the fulfillment of the actual situation of life, the complete presence of the reality in which one participates" (1965:97). This presence entails an ingathering of the other's presence, by "that subterranean dialogic, that steady potential presence. . . . Then there is reality *between* them, there is mutuality" (1965:98).

Through this presence, the teacher—or "educator" in Buber's term—represents both the opening and the emanation of vital cultural traditions, for which concrete presence, or being, enables the child or student to "receive," in kabbalistic (or, for Buber, Hasidic) imagery. He writes:

> Yet the master remains the model for the teacher. For if the educator of our day has to act consciously he must nevertheless do it "as though he did not." That raising of the finger, that questioning glance, are his genuine doing. . . . the selection of the effective world must be *concentrated* in him; and doing out of concentration has the appearance of rest . . . but a hidden influence proceeding from his integrity has an integrating force. (1965:90)

Integration and unity, concentration and fullness rather than separation, diffusion and emptiness are the goals of such a conscious/unconscious educational interaction. In this version of "character education," there is an "education for community," but not the collective internalization of shared values that typifies contemporary discussions. Instead, Buber observed:

> The mass of contradictions can be met and conquered only by the rebirth of personal unity, *unity of being,* unity of life, unity of action—unity of being, life and action together. . . . It is the longing for personal unity from which must be born a unity of mankind, which the educator should lay hold of and strengthen in his pupils. (1965:116)

For us, this longing is, of course, at first a compensatory desire, a residual effect of the reorganization of self that takes place in the culture of the postindustrial workplace (Casey, 1995). The desire for presence and unified being, for mutuality and dialogical relation grows only with the evident failures of corporate recodings and revivals of a shattered self, an emptiness encased by rigidified shells that are nourished by consumption of the "ten thousand things." Creativity, which Buber calls the "instinct of origination," is an antidote to the false solution of "having," because it "never becomes greed, because it is not directed to 'having', but only to doing" (1965:87). This doing is the as-though-not-conscious naturalness of being, the same doing/being that Fromm opposed to the alienated market consumerism of "having" (Fromm, 1976).

One implication for an educational movement that is not merely oppositional or marginally corrective, but creatively different, is to cultivate that being of presence which is the existential, at first apparently individual and subjective, alternative to a devitalized (do we really believe that "chronic fatigue syndrome" is an entirely intrapersonal, physiological phenomenon?), performance-structured, commodity-oriented, decaying, postmodern self. The new age cultural wave makes possible (just as it may also limit) not only an initially narcissistic resubjectification, but also a deeper cultural shift of basic premises, as Pitirim Sorokin (1957) argued. In turn, a new vocabulary and consciousness that can reverberate in social theory and education offers a new cultural foundation for both social theory and education.

For teaching, as for the revitalization of everyday social life, there is no protocol or formula for being. But our emphasis here on the sociocultural conditions or context for changes in social theory and education—the refusal of a postmodern antihistory—does not deny intentionality, which is the directed action of Hasidic sanctification of everyday life that Buber so much praised as different from the rabbinic, legal rationalist Judaism of the European mainstream. The emphasis on presence or being in education, and in teaching especially, is not spontaneism, but a sort of Taoist conscious naturalness that Buber idealized in the teacher as master. While not routine, this ideal does imply disciplined practice or, in Western terms, "virtue."

Fromm's posthumously published (1994) book, *The Art of Being*, represents a condensed effort to catalog such disciplined practices that could realize an alternative to the alienated, consumer-driven culture and self against which he struggled in all of his work. Fromm offers a short road map to what he had earlier (Fromm, 1976) called a "city of being." His insights into practicing being are drawn not only from a socialist critique of what we now call postmodern society, or a psychoanalytic background and commitment to rational demystification, or even a radical reading of the Old Testament as a blueprint for an historical, collective path toward a nonidolatrous, dealienated social existence. Drawing upon so-called Eastern religions and what are unmistakably instances of new age "bodywork," Fromm offers an outline of practices that could well constitute a different path of teacher formation, based on a different sociocultural premise.

What I am suggesting is not only that this reconceptualized practice of virtue—these "arts of being"—is of general interest for the transformation of social interaction and individual identity, but also that as a schematic catalog it offers an alternative model for "educating the educator." These "arts of being" suggest the possibility of a curriculum of teacher education that is different than the traditional, industrial-bureaucratic teacher education, with its interest in transmission of the rules and regulation of pedagogy and disciplinary subjects. The *presence* of the educator also suggests a different path than the current postindustrial education curriculum emphasis on managed forms of collaboration that blur institutional boundaries, and thereby further corporatist social forms of regulation and governance. This new alternative curriculum also stands in contrast to a so-called radical, slogan-like authoritarianism that parades under the banner of "critical pedagogy" in both modern and postmodern forms.

This entirely different training of educators is a training for being, for presence, for the concentrated intelligence of awareness that enables inclusion of the other side—the student—as an organic, living being and not as an object of mechanical or electronic desire for control and manipulation in the name of performance standards, new skills, and personal and national success in global competition. Are these latter terms not the watchwords of contemporary educational change around the postindustrial, postmodern world? For subjective and culturally creative revitalization the teacher has, first of all, to be alive, not dead. I have argued that a generative source for this resubjectification is in a broader cultural revitalization, one that flows from a transcendental mediation of intersubjectivity, and that rationalizes and elaborates world views deriving from renewals of ancient symbolic traditions of the sacred.

Although Fromm secularizes his catalog of the arts of being, these arts develop historically as cultural integrals and are most fully expressed in religious or sacred aspects of those historic, core civilizational cultures. Like the soul traveler of Dante's Inferno, Fromm's seeker of "attaining optimal being," must pass through the "suggestion apparatus of society," which produces the "inner chains" that block both inner and outer liberation (1994:4-10). Socially produced obstacles to liberation are the "great shams" of promises of power and fame, excessive cerebral orientation, and the illusions, including the illusion of what we are calling new age cultural practices (1994:11). Fromm already foresaw commodification of forces for the "transformation from within." He warned of what he referred to as the "commercialization of the salvation business": "Has the spirit of big business and its selling methods already made such inroads that one must also accept them in the field of individual spiritual development?" (1994:17).

Fromm poses an alternative, drawing on Eastern traditions for disciplined practices designed to shed illusions, in much the same way as Csikszentmihalyi (1993) offers a cognitive psychological evolutionary theory of attention. Here too, the key is the cultivation of awareness. Fromm writes:

> The conclusion from all these considerations is that the most important step in the art of being is everything that leads to and enhances our capacity for heightened awareness and, as far as the mind is concerned, for critical, questioning thinking. (1994:43)

He also uses the language of energy in discussing awareness, concentration and the goal of revitalization: "Mobilization of energy, which has a psychic as well as a physiological aspect, has the effect of making one feel alive" (1994:45).

Buber and Fromm coalesce in the emphasis on concentration and attending to the presence of the other as a formative, necessary element of any intersubjectivity: "the Buddhist concept of *mindfulness* [emphasis added] means precisely a way of being in which one is fully concentrated on everything one is doing at any given moment" (1994:49). This ideal of integration of attention is quite different from the superficial, postmodern celebration of noisy, carnivalesque polyvocality.

Concentrated, mindful presence is a protection against the attachment of energies to a mode of dependent submission to powerful others, which is now identified as idolatry (alienation). For even in a psychoanalytically oriented secularization of sacred disciplines of being, Fromm intersperses the more culturally foundational vocabularies drawn from traditions of collectively organized, subjective sacred experience. Fromm aims to cultivate cognitive, rational, intersubjective presence in his recollected arts of being. He wants to resuscitate the feeling, "affect," that has been severed from intellection. This severance of feeling blocks the vitalizing experience of joy, and the capacity for what Jessica Benjamin (1988) and Buber both call "mutuality," but which Fromm refers to simply as the "capacity for giving," and, as we have seen, "for loving." "In summary," he writes: "modern man *has* many things and uses many things, but he *is* very little. His feelings and thinking processes are atrophied like unused muscles (1994:96). Here the echo of Marx's theory of alienation (see Bertell Ollman, 1971) is very loud.

Postmodern idolatry is consumption, having, trying to fill the emptiness with food, devouring sex, and other manifestations of "hostile possessiveness." In the end, culturally and religiously derived, individuated practices of being can change identity: "To sum up once more: Awareness, will, practice, tolerance of fear and new experience, they are all necessary if transformation of the individual is to succeed" (Fromm, 1994:120).

Teaching in Sociocultural Movement

Fromm's educative interest in culling and communicating eclectic practices to transform identity and society certainly can provide a basis for creating an alternative curriculum for teacher education. Transformative teaching requires that the teacher herself or himself be fully whole, and sufficiently aware to respond concretely to the student, opening a dialogic path for individual growth and development. In a time when mechanical petrification pervades teacher-student interaction, the existential emphasis on awareness is a mild corrective.

Indeed, Fromm's catalog is easily assimilable to new age cultural trends, commercialized and otherwise. In part, this is because the arts of being are consistently separated from any of their generative sources. Putting it severely, they are desocialized and decultured, appearing as interactional devices, interpersonal knacks that can obstruct a much larger apparatus working to inhibit the development of full human being. Despite the intention, the effect is to separate and extricate the individual from society, culture, history, and dynamic closeness to such energizing approaches to the sacred that we have touched upon. While I do think that an orientation to a dialogic teaching of presence is a salutary corrective to the educational trends that we have described and that the arts of being can be fruitfully brought to teacher education, still, as decultured devices, they are ironically alienated from the broader sociocultural movements within which educational change is contained.

Resacralizing teaching, as a revitalizing alternative to postmodern educational forms in both corporatism and its critiques, can avoid the very commercialization that Fromm feared only by itself being integral to a larger, dynamic whole. Practically, the expression of resacralized social forms is much more evident in socioeducational activities less institutionalized than teaching (in its current professionalized organization). Such oppositional resacralization would require a deprofessionalization and debureaucratization of teaching to the extent that teaching could become a personal "calling" to actualize the transformation of identity.

While Weber (1946) railed against ersatz prophecy in the university lecture hall, simultaneously he described prophetic styles as dynamic elements in historic transformation. Indeed, one of the responsibilities that intellectuals had forsaken was the work of rationalizing and sublimating religious salvation ethics. Weber's (1958) typology of prophecy does show an example of how resacralized teaching can become a socially dynamic force.

Without intersubjectivity, teaching from within cultural movements becomes the sort of collectivist "box of scorpions" that Buber shunned in his anticentralist utopian socialism. Yet, without contextualization in sociocultural movement, any arts-of-being, new age, or resacralized teaching becomes, despite its advance on the present, an individualized interaction device to produce student-workers as arrays of surface or flexible skill performers.

I suggest then, a combination of teaching with styles of prophecy, as a heuristic way of underlining the sociocultural embeddedness of any durable effective teaching. This no more means that all teachers should become prophets (sacralized "transformative intellectuals") than does my attempt to resacralize social theory and education as explanation indicate a predilection for religious schools, as currently constituted. Rather, it is a simultaneous recognition of the historic sociocultural preeminence of religion and an effort to revitalize decadent cultural, theoretical and educational ways of thinking and being. It is a method of breaking out of current ways of thinking about teaching.

This interest in prophecy is found in Weber's juxtaposition of prophet and priest, and the educational analogues for deinstitutionalizing routine or "priestly" teaching, in favor of an enlivening, engaging "prophetic" teaching. Weber indicates the difference:

> For our purposes here, the personal call is the decisive element distinguishing the prophet from the priest. The latter lays claim to authority by virtue of his service in a sacred tradition, while the prophet's claim is based on personal revelation and charisma. (1964:46)

Weber differentiates the prophet from founders of schools of philosophy, teachers of ethics, and even those traditionally classed as prophets whom he categorizes as theorists of social reform. What does link teachers and prophets is the strength of the bond between a teacher of religious or philosophical wisdom and his disciple. But, what finally differentiates prophets from other teachers is not the reverence of the "disciple-master relationship", but teachers' "lack of that vital emotional preaching which is distinctive of prophecy" (Weber, 1964:52,53). It is then hyperbolic to suggest that teachers can, or should, become more like prophets as sociocultural and educational sacralization increases. But, the exaggeration does underline both the necessity of emotional bonding and the integration of teaching within a living cultural tradition that feeds organic social, individuated identities. These are elements that are barely present in the contemporary model of education, which posits flexible standards and performance-accountability.

To state the analytical interest even more baldly, if Bernstein's sociology is a recontextualization of Durkheim's sociology of religion, at a cultural time of resacralization movements, should we not ask what other sociologies of religion, such as Weber's, imply for a social understanding of education? Further, without advocating religious schools, should we not ask more, following our larger analytic pattern of reading sociology back into culture and culture into religion, about the implications of religious theory and practice for creating new models of educational theory and practice?

So, for example, Weber's types of ethical and exemplary prophecy offer clues to understanding different types of teaching—first, as modes of interaction, but then more generally, as analyses of individual being, teaching practice and cultural movement. These are very different sorts of linked analyses: an ethical prophecy of obligatory correction of action according to abstract norms; and an exemplary prophecy that does not preach ethical obligation, but "rather directs itself to the self-interest of those who crave salvation, recommending to them the same path as he himself traversed" (Weber, 1964:55).

According to this resacralized approach, teaching would be seen more as a cultural practice aligned with other institutional practices. The social effect of postindustrialism in production and postmodernism in consumption has been a blurring of practices and meanings across sectors of society. This reversal, if not of the division of labor in fact, then of its representations, is heightened also by current resacralization movements which, commercialized, authoritarian or not, aim to reduce boundaries between the sacred and profane. Just as changing production and communication technologies and organizational devices migrate to the educational sector, so too does a changed cultural premise and practice inevitably press for expression in various forms of resacralized education.

The resacralization of culture means, theoretically, a rethinking of education in terms of religion, to the extent that the sociocultural foundations of education are resacralized. Theoretically, it implies the borrowing and adaptation of categories such as ethical and exemplary prophecy in order to understand changes in teaching and to be able to contextualize those changes in wider sociocultural movements. Practically, it means a new complement to the postindustrial press for educational restructuring. The interesting analytical issue is precisely the interaction of these apparently contradictory tendencies: postindustrialism and resacralization. Perhaps the most apparent manifestation of the effects of this interaction is the comfort of religious, politically rightist groups with corporatist school reform. On a subtler side of the social realignment process, religious groups interested in education join the liberal and libertarian communalists, who may demur from economic education reform as excessive instrumentalism in the name of remoralization and character education.

These contradictions are not going to be resolved theoretically, but in political, social, cultural educational practice and movement. What is possible is that these sociocultural movements can at least be attended to by social theorists of education, since they may provide an opportunity to move paradigmatically into more open space. From this place we look away from an ever more strident critical sociology of education and an appropriately superficial and fragmented collaging of postmodern icons and aesthetics to social analyses of education.

Instead, there is now an opening toward the religious foundations of culture, which reappear, subject both to a fundamentalist appropriation and to a contemporary revisionist reading. This revisionism is fused with a socially transformative interest in a revolutionary renewal of theory and practice in society and education.

Chapter Seven

Holy Sparks and Social Explanation

"Ascent of the Soul"

Ezekiel's vision of the chariot's ascent to the throne of heaven (Scholem, 1974) offers not only a heavenly cartography for the earliest Jewish mystics, but also a model of individual development, an ecstatically driven movement of individual transformation. As Allen Afterman (1992), Moshe Idel (1988) and, in a different, more rationalist key, Emmanuel Levinas (1994) all emphasize, the soul's ascent—the drawing down of the supernal emanation of light and the coming closer, the "cleaving" communion with the divine—is deeply integrative of experiential and textual practices. Idel shows in great historical detail the distinct differences among textually oriented "theurgic" and experientially oriented "ecstatic" strands in the history of the kabbalist movement. Yet, it is Idel who observes, in a discussion of kabbalistic hermeneutics, what is worth quoting again:

> In Jewish medieval Kabbalistic traditions, as in Hasidism, there is clear evidence supporting the conclusion that pneumatic experiences are viewed as a prelude to a particular kind of literary activity—biblical exegesis. (1988:243)

In turn, this exegesis—Torah study—is understood to induce mystical, ecstatic transcendental states and experiences if undertaken with proper intention and practical guidance. The transformation of identity that Erich Fromm (1976) reaches for in a new "city of being" is the result of an integration of textual, interpretive work and meditative reshaping of experienced consciousness: of being and knowing, in Levinas's (1994) "translation into Greek" of his Talmudic readings; or, what we have called "recontextualization."

The secular theory/practice relation is illuminated by this resacralization of our work process. The integrative insistence is particularly relevant to critical postmodern theories of society and education that, in practice, have separated social theorizing about education not only from observation or engagement with prevailing mundane instances of educational practice in schools, for example, but also—and perhaps more importantly—from the theorist's practice on herself or himself.

This separation replicates the wider alienation that is a central topic of critical theory. It enables the creation of theoretical products that come out of a routinized life process, thereby denying in their very "mode of production" the creative renewal. These theoretical products also deny the difficulty of the attempt to live life not in fragmentary idolatry, but in the light of an infinitude that is not separated from this world.

The integration of perception in the present with something outside-the-present is the method of present transformation. The resources to activate this capacity for living the present in the light of eternity—and thereby transforming its limiting, evil, centrifugal and entropic processes—exist already in the world. The possibility of reaching these resources requires the intentional, human intervention that can redeem the capacity for an optimal social condition. This is the time before the two trees of life and knowledge came apart from their common source in descended energy.

The descended energy, as I have indicated from all the secondary sources following the Creation account of the Lurianic Kabbalah, is present in the potentialities of being that are activated by a range of traditional practices. These practices include not only ecstatic states or revolutionary hermeneutics (in Scholem's account, 1971:282-303), but also the ethical behavior that Levinas (1994:47) equates with Revelation, and that requires such practices ("arts") of being for their realization, which is the reparation of this everyday, intersubjective world. Scholem writes:

> And this is not all. Into the deep abyss of the forces of evil, the forces of darkness and impurity which the Kabbalists call "shells"

> or "offscourings," there fell as a result of the breaking of the vessels, forces of holiness, sparks of divine light. Hence, there is a Galut (exile) of the divine itself, of the "sparks of the Shekhinah": "These sparks of holiness are bound in fetters of steel in the depth of the shells, and yearningly aspire to rise to their source but cannot avail to do so until they have support"—so says Rabbi Hayyim Vital, a disciple of Luria. (1971:45)

What the growing legitimacy of cultural resacralization offers to a truly *post* modern critical social theory of education is precisely the renewal in theory and in the relation between theory and practice that wider sociocultural movements claim for culture. This renewal, however, requires a "will to surrender" or, as Afterman (1992:56) terms it, "the will to openness." Support for this surrender is self-augmenting, enhanced by a willingness to let go of vocabularies of social theory that we have come to think of as objective and scientific ("bound in fetters of steel"), rather than as deeply routinized rationalizations of historic cultural movements. In the case of sociology, I have built on the argument that its conceptual apparatus reflects a secularization of the cosmology of "innerworldy asceticism," to use Weber's familiar term.

Such redirection of vocabulary is facilitated by cultural processes. These processes can be resacralized or secular, commodified and commercialized or marginal and organic; they press beyond the asceticism of early industrial modernity, through the consumption-oriented narcissism of postindustrialism's first phase, to a highly individuated, but communal search for self-regulating practices. These are practices that use otherworldliness to maximize the this-worldly desires for satisfaction generated by the apparatus's need for a progressive, self-sustaining increase in consumption. The incorporative use of otherworldliness as an outside loop that boosts the apparatus's power in production and consumption by specifying and adapting the individual subject has, however, as an unintended consequence the effect that the closed and sealed domain of the sacred has been reopened. Innerworldly mysticism is rekindled as the commercialization of salvation burns away the insulation of the sacred from the profane and revolutionary charismatic yearnings are inflamed.

The incorporative social method of utilizing these formerly external, sacred cultural resources within the productive system apparatus as a mode of apparently manageable individuated practices of subject self-regulation has numerous effects, two of which I have tried to articulate. Premodern traditions of sacred knowledge become accessible to mass consumption. These traditions have possibilities for cultural and theoretical innovation. Resacralization, however intertwined are its roots with the current phase of a global, capitalist, postindustrial apparatus, has as an effect the reinforcement of an unusual hybrid, one that Max Weber identified largely logically rather than fully empirically in his canonical sociology of religion: innerworldly mysticism.

Innerworldly Mysticism

So, critical theory is sacralized, opening the sealed coffins of esoteric ancestors with a hope for revivification in the revision of dissenting traditions that appear applicable to the innerworldly transformative task of the present. Weber, in his critical sociology of modern industrialism, did not foresee the potentialities of any such innerwordly mysticism. He was consistent in his attribution of the cultural foundations of the modern, bureaucratic, rationalist apparatus to ascetic Protestantism. Weber writes:

> This inner-worldly asceticism had a number of distinctive consequences not found in any other religion. . . . The clear and uniform goal of this asceticism was the disciplining and methodical organization of the whole pattern of life. Its typical representative was the "man of a vocation," and its unique result was the rational organization and institutionalization of social relationships. (1964:183)

The polarity to asceticism is contemplation or mysticism. Weber is convinced that such contemplative, ecstatic mysticism generally does not engage this world, and certainly not in a socially transformative direction. There are exceptions, mentioned briefly, for example: "The transformation of a mysticism remote from the world into one characterized by chiliastic and revolutionary tendencies took place frequently, most impressively in the revolutionary mysticism of the sixteenth-century Baptists" (1964:175). But, he follows quickly with the reassertion of the socially quietistic consequences of contemplative rather than ascetic mysticism: "To the extent that an inner-worldly religion of salvation is determined by contemplative features, the usual result is acceptance of the secular social structure" (1964:175). And, elsewhere, in his essay "The Social Psychology of the World Religions," he is even more emphatic in his claim that asceticism must be the religious cultural foundation: "In their innermost beings, contemplative and ecstatic religions have been rather specifically hostile to economic life" (1946:289).

Our point is that this religious, innerworldly ascetic foundation of modern culture has been transmuting to an innerworldly, ecstatic, contemplative or mystical orientation. While this emergent social ethic is generally integrated into the maintenance of a postindustrial and culturally postmodern apparatus, its effects are multilineal and—most importantly—set the cultural horizon for a very different range of potential sociocultural movements and social forms. Innerworldly mysticism, like the postmodern tendency that precedes and prepares it, depends on the erasure of boundaries and not on the Weberian and Habermasian modern autonomy of separate spheres. That is a transitional value of postmodern culture, seen as a decadent phase of modernity and ancillary to postindustrial production, distribution, communication and institutional restructuring.

The practical examples offered—of twelve-step revivalism, or baby-boom religion, or even the "culture of narcissism," more generally—are only signs of what I hypothesize as a much broader mass cultural tendency: the resubjectification and resymbolization, following narcissism, toward innerworldly mysticism as the religious foundation of new age and late postmodern culture. We have been exploring the social theoretical and educational implications of such a resacralization. My point here is that esoteric and Eastern religious traditions provide such grounds for contemporary theory and practice.

Against Weber, at least the current historical conjuncture indicates the possibility of an innerworldly mysticism that is socially interested rather than merely accepting and quietistic and that goes beyond the symbolic reintegration of communities toward a socially transformative ethic grounded in the erasure of the difference between sacred and profane. The later kabbalistic movements, if one may so describe Hasidism, are, I believe, a precursory example at the theoretical level, if not always even necessarily in practice. We should not follow eighteenth-century European Hasidism as a social-movement example. Rather, I suggest a conceptual paradigm that may be relevant to contemporary transformative movements, both as a theoretical exemplar and in practice.

Kabbalistic movements first are different than the "flight from the world" that Weber ascribes to nonascetic, mystical religions in their socially redemptive messianism. As Scholem argued, this is not a linear, progressive messianism, later claimed as a secularization in Europe as an aspect of the Enlightenment. Rather, it is discontinuous, and as our discussion of kabbalistic time indicated, redemption is linked to the decisive and, in Buber's term "incessant renewal" of the moment. Despite the use (shared with many other esoteric traditions) of mystical practices of letters, numbers and shapes as techniques in meditation or contemplation in "ascent," there is repeated emphasis on "other-oriented action," required active performance of ethical behavior, and the perpetual overcoming of the gap between being and knowing. This is the integration of the two trees to their common root in the primordial Garden.

If this specific tradition and others like it in Christianity, Buddhism, Hinduism, and Islam (see, for an overview, Merkur, 1993) now speak to the avatars of a new culture, then Weber's typology is mistaken, not in a typological sense, but now empirically. A new religiocultural foundation now seen as innerworldly asceticism does not mean social passivity. Further, the inapplicability of the ascetic/contemplative split to kabbalism is observed independently by Scholem in his description connecting communion, or "devekut," to cleaving: "Devekut is a value of contemplative, not active life. But Nahmanides' saying could be used to prove the possibility of the *coincidence of the two spheres* [emphasis added]" (1971:205). For Buber, of course, the commitment to such a coincidence or erasure of boundaries is not merely a possibility, but rather the Hasidic goal of hallowing the everyday, sanctifying—and so transforming—the holy sparks of transcendental being out of the "encased in steel" covering of the present profane moment. So too, the emergent cultural premise is an active, socially oriented innerworldly mysticism. Its presence in the world, perhaps unlike the lofty intentionality of kabbalistic harmonious world reparation, may be linked more directly to the reproduction of postindustrially specified selves as labor power (Casey, 1995) and more to the satisfaction of narcissistic desire than to the messianic hunger and drive for redemption.

Yet, the effect may be quite similar: culturally prescribed, individuated practices of contemplative self-transformation that first are oriented to social relational ideals in micro, self-other interaction. The effects of a social innerworldly mysticism would likely include meso levels of community-building and macro-level social transformation as various as ecological apocalypses. This ethic entails new age rituals like "harmonic convergences" (celestial alignments) as well as communitarian conferences.

This is the emergent ground upon which a simultaneously sacred and secular new culture becomes increasingly apparent. The self that appears in this new culture will encompass many different qualities, some of them seemingly contradictory. It will be both contemplative and active; male and female; disciplined, but not self-denying; temporally aware and open; experimentally delineated; individual and collective. With this new subjectivity will also come fundamental changes in the character of social theory and educational practice.

"The Other Side"

My purpose here has been to set out a background for such work and to try to show what the cultural and theoretical process looks like that leads to this new stage. Further, I have explored one esoteric tradition as an example of sacralized social theory. Finally, I have tried to draw some broad-stroke implications of cultural and social theoretic resacralization tendencies for resacralized education.

All this goes against the grain of both current educational practices and the directions of their reform, as well as social theory generally, and social theory in education, particularly. In educational practice, postindustrialism is the pressing insurgent force, working to "break the mold" of factory schools in order to successfully prepare workers for reorganized postindustrial workplaces. All the terms of postindustrial education are not yet in place. The factory school will hang on, especially in the most economically underdeveloped regions within and without the world centers of corporate capital concentration, cultural trend setting, and political and military leadership. These latter political and military priorities may well slow the pace of investment in educational reform, but will not forestall what now appears inevitable. The factory school, and its broader apparatus of social pedagogy, is dead. Welcome to the corporate, corporatist, postindustrial school and its wider educational regime.

In social theory, the traditional autonomy of spheres between sociology and the wider culture remains. The technologically driven implosion of information onto even the individual nodes of the World Wide Web makes it more difficult and less profitable in the publishing industry for even American sociologists to ignore the pervasive discourse of postmodernism. This now becomes the hegemonic language, in high, academicized culture, as well as in mass culture, as a practice, and to the second derivative degree, as a cultural-studies reflection on mass culture.

Routinization of broader cultural languages of postmodern cultural studies and institutionalization of belated efforts to reduce gender and race caste stratification in the academy, all point to continuing change in social theory; a move toward deeper immersion in postmodern culture, at least at an academically reflexive, second remove.

In these conditions, I find it pressing to try to rationally articulate countertendencies and the possibilities that I see as emergent for social theory and education. The vaunted "otherness" of contemporary postmodern critical social theory is so much more of the same. Yet, I do not believe that the resacralization of culture—and its social theoretical and educational aspects—is an artificial otherness, an artifactual difference fabricated to maintain the differentiation process itself (though I admit to seeing the systemic apparatus utility in that as well). What I have done, then, is to outline the argument of the link between religion, culture, social theory and education and try to specify it with examples from contemporary sociocultural movements as well as classical modern social theories (read in their subtexts) and dissident, Romantic and esoteric religious traditions.

This sacred sociocultural tendency does not erase the major hegemonic tendency, which is not simply social rationalization but intensified monetization of dynamic connections among all social relations and bonds and their formation as commodities. Secularization, seen in this monetizing and commodifying way, is still not realized. James Coleman (1993) correctly follows this social logic out to the monetization of child and parent, child and state relations. So, in the bigger picture, the resacralization tendency is really the "other side." Here, however, I reverse the emphasis to underline the emergent cultural importance of the sacred. But then I also want to indicate that it is still only the alternative to the main social posture.

Religious Theory

There is much more work to be done along these broad lines. Theoretically, even the kabbalistic exposition can be much deepened, and Jewish scholars will not be happy with my selective borrowings and condensations. More generally, while I do see the universal aspirations in that particular example both for its practitioners and for me as a removed reflexive cultural borrower, the wider field of work that I see before us is a rereading of all the esoteric religious traditions, from a contemporary point of view, and, ideally, from the vantage point of a critical social interest. Not only the religious margins, but also the mainstream can be reread with the recontextualizing license that postmodern eclecticism has permitted.

Still, I do see the especially rich potentialities in a *social* reading of the Eastern traditions, in part because they have been so little used as a resource for what are admittedly the hegemonic Eurocentric religiocultural roots of social theory, including critical theory. My argument has been that these are not bibliographical decisions, but cultural imperatives that begin to make intellectual sense as the basic premises of culture change. In the language of another tradition: carpe diem.

Social History

I have not provided anything like a full social analytic description of new age culture, not because I do not value such empirical social description, but because I want to press the social theoretic and educational practice points now, even in advance of what I predict will be a further flowering of this cultural emergent and much detailed description and analysis by many interested social inquirers. Likewise, the recent roots of these cultural expressions in the so-called consciousness revolution of the 1960s have not been traced, although I believe that they can and will be studied.

In critical social theory, the suppression of European Marxism had been so profound in the United States that the "cultural revolution" in its academic aspect drew upon the critical political economic paradigms that had been absent, as well as Left Marxists' psychoanalytical and cultural interests. Interest in the expansion and self-regulation of consciousness may have grown since that time. It is now realized much more extensively in new age publishing and adult educational institutions. But, the academic rationalization of this aspect of the sixties social movements never occurred. Richard Alpert became

Ram Dass, a recognizable figure of new age culture, but no critical social theory followed the consciousness revolution back behind the immediate, mechanical gratification of addictive desire to the organic traditions of Eastern religions, either as text or as practice. Instead, poststructuralism—and later, postmodernism—became the counterpoint to a political economy–based "new sociology of education." Culture was rediscovered, followed quickly by a linked interest in postmodern culture and culture studies. Yet, no theoretical grounding was sought for this interest beyond secular, European social philosophy.

Events in social history brought an alternative sociocultural foundation for social theory and for education to the fore. Yet even this intellectual appropriation of this recent history is still seen as idiosyncratic. What I have done in this book is to try to take that path of theoretical appropriation, recontextualization and recoding of sociocultural movement. What I have not done is to document this cultural shift historically, connecting new age culture, as I suggest here, to the consciousness revolution of the 1960s and to its popular and academic paths in recent social history.

Social Physics

My allusions to a thematic of energy, both in the subtexts and precursors of modern social theory, are at a very general, and physically empirically unsubstantiated, level. While I chose to emphasize a series of cultural transformations, my interest in the material, physicochemical meaning of energy in relation to social interaction is undeniable. Recent Japanese laboratory research on the biochemistry of bodily energy—under the rubric of classical Chinese physiology's concept of "chi"—centers on showing how environmental, social alterations can be related to various measures of bodily energy. Yasuo Yuasa's (1993) work represents a powerful effort to assimilate Japanese martial arts, Eastern medicine, and physiological psychology in a "science of ki-energy," as part of his mind-body theory. Similarly, despite controversy surrounding them, mind-body practices are now topics of mass Western interest and even medical acknowledgment (by signs such as establishment of an alternative-medicine research branch at the U.S. National Institutes of Health). The centrality of the mind-body question and its formulation in energy terms in the current mass vernaculars of new age self-help is evident even in a casual perusal of sales in mass-distribution bookstores.

From energy to holy sparks, there is a pervasive vitalism in new age culture and in the antecedents or earlier parallels that I describe. This is not to advocate a simple material reduction of either the importance of the life-against-death imagery so clearly expressed by Norman Brown (1959) or of the effects of the search and experience of textual and ecstatic innerworldly mysticism's infinitude and "cleaving." The Hasidic "quickening," Emile Durkheim's "warm" "electricity," and even perhaps Wilhelm Reich's "bions" have their own efficacious level of reality. It is tempting, however, to equate bions with Yogic "prana" and kabbalistic "sefirot" with Hindu "chakras" and Chinese "chi" and to suggest that the "hayyut" and the aliveness of libido share a common physiological process and stratum (see, for example, Yuasa, 1993).

Such a biochemical reduction is not my interest nor within my scope. Suffice it to say that the pervasiveness of this theme is not easily denied. While our interest is in a sense in the subjective aspect of cultural energy or capacity and in the relation of such cultural potence to socially structured transcendental perception, we must see that a very different sort of "sociobiology," for social theory and research, is implied by the cultural tendency of resacralization and the larger world of theoretical resources that it unearths.

Religious and Political Fundamentalism

I mention Jonestown and Waco—and could have added Tokyo, Switzerland and Oklahoma City—as examples of charismatic reaction to rationalization run amok. Weber's own relation to this dynamic polarity is notoriously ambivalent. He feared the mechanical petrification of the iron cage that secularized Protestant asceticism had become in the spirit of capitalism and in the alienating bureaucratic apparatus. Yet, he was disdainful of unrationalized experience and ersatz prophecy, and, like Marx, recognized societal rationalization as also an historical advance.

I have taken the charismatic aspect and tried to run with it, both for analytical and political reasons. Analytically, I react against what I perceive as an unfruitful routinization of contemporary social theoretic resources in postmodern critical social theory. Amplifying the cultural charismatic and sacralizing possibility legitimates the exploration of religious theories as a method for the revitalization of what I see as currently theoretically ossified. Politically, the foreclosing power of commodification and incorporative apparatuses seems so great (standard of living benefits not withstanding) that enlivening, vivifying openings for realization of human capacities, for "optimal being," seem narrow relative to the pervasive deadening logic of the general system.

Even from within the apparatus, the promise of the fulfillment of desire is evidently not achieved by further intensifying well-known institutional ideals and organizational practices of rationalization. Alienation and mechanical petrification are dangers familiar to the new class stratum in the new age culture, the carriers of social theory and policies of educational practice whose specialized task is, of course, rationalization.

None of this awareness or commitment precludes fear of an unleashed religiously legitimated, mass expression of a deregulated mass social irrationality: new age fascism. I see the ingathering of the holy sparks as a new renaissance and a new "enlightenment," as the uplifting of our eyes, away from rationalized, steel-encasing dross to the light of an illuminating and humanizing experience of a divinely loving and love-inducing eternal infinitude. Yet, I rightly fear that these also may be sparks of conflagration and that what is being gathered in and concentrated are particularistic forces of ignorance, hatred, prejudice and a love only of violence and self-hating destruction, displaced into the violent murder of the collective other.

Resurgent nationalism and new forms of insularizing particularism are brought to the surface, along with buried sacred traditions, as the embodied legitimacy of modern Enlightenment in high and mass culture gives way to fetishisms of antiobjects and antifeelings born out of postmodern desperation for breathing space within the arid machine. This is a shorter, more pallid version of the central irrational narrative of our age, the Holocaust.

There is a murderous seesaw, between excessive profanation and convulsive sacralization. Each side needs to be humanized. Here I do not put forward a humanist program, except to say that even in the very moment of amplifying the irrational and in rationalizing the sacred, the other side is denied at the cost of now historically well-known sacrifices of human life. In seeing a transformative possibility for social theory and educational practice in revision of premodern, sacred traditions, I do not forget the past or the present danger of socially rationalized collective irrationality, a negative unification of both sides that we remember in the Holocaust. Waco is a different destructive unity of both sides. It represents a dialectic of destruction in the interaction of mindless bureaucratic rationalism and irrational, transcendental sacrificial authoritarianism. Beyond the polarities and forced unities, there remains still unexplored in our discussion the theory and practice of a social intersubjectivity, a social interaction that does not split to biochemistry and theosophy, but is simultaneously humanizing, by virtue of its sacred aspiration.

Social Interaction and Education

Gershom Scholem and Martin Buber may disagree about Hasidism, about the historical accuracy of relative weightings of textualism and ecstaticism, of concrete immediacy and rational, albeit Gnostic, reflection. But, questions of Hasidic sanctification of the quotidian encourage other questions about sacralizing social movements—questions about the authoritarianism of the "pious ones," the mediators of divine influx and innerworldly libido, and their feudal courts of tribute. Kabbalistic theories of the Godhead are deeply sexual, and as in other esoteric traditions, the receptive power of the feminine is idealized. Yet, even in recent interpretations, nothing is asked about feminine equality in sacred practice.

Also unanswered for us are questions about both Hasidism and Buber's existentialist appropriation with regard to the extent of transcendental mediation of intersubjectivity. Reversing the question, we do not know the impact of new age sacralizing movement on the development of human intersubjectivty. Emmanuel Levinas (1994:170) is suspicious of intersubjectivity outside the law, an intersubjective social relation overly reliant on the immediate insights of "spirit" rather than on communally regulated objective commandments of the law and its letter.

As he puts this more Durkheimian, more rabbinic, rationally oriented model of intersubjective distrust of existentialism: "One cannot be less attached to the letter and more enamored of the spirit" (1994:19).

Our approach to social interaction, in its cultural borrowings, has emphasized, new age–like, the spirit rather than the letter, perception and consciousness more than rite and traditional regulation of social behavior. Resacralization in a social theory of interaction has this other side of ritual and law, which we have neglected here in order to explore what I see as the historically underrepresented interest in the irrational as a basis for social interaction, not simply as libidinal cathexis or transferred attachment, but as an emotionally based social interaction that draws motivational energy from transcendental belief and quest. Future exploration of intersubjectivity will, I hope, go beyond the corrective to an attempt to theorize both sides simultaneously.

Even the emphasis on social interaction in education is a departure. New sociology of education was directed to macrostructural social processes and, only recently, to cultural questions. While I have tried to place the cultural, theoretical and educational discussions within a wider social frame, the interest here in a cultural and interactional approach can be taken as a forgetting of political economic and class questions and larger macrosocial questions. Clearly, the analysis of the social reorganization of schooling in corporatism fits that traditional social analytic interest. What is less evident, in part because it is less expressly elaborated here, is that it is precisely the macrosocial analysis that leads us to an increased attention to intersubjectivity in education. The intensified rationalization and stratification of education is what makes an intersubjective approach transformatively relevant. Yet, specification of that macrostructural other side is only indirectly achieved by an interactional, cultural, and religious emphasis.

Social Explanation

If pneumatic exegesis is our exemplar and the surpassing of basic dualisms such as ecstasy and law our ideal, then it must be understood that practical fullness of being as an antidote to mechanically petrifying alienation is not presented to displace rational social understanding or explanation. The sort of esotericism that I use to reassert the sacred is one which always wishes to "return" from where it has been. Like Rabbi Akiva, in the legend of those who perish through death and madness on the path of ascent, ours is the singular choice to return to this descended world, which permits other-oriented action and which requires reparation by interpretation and ethical action (Levinas, 1994).

My hope is to revise social explanation in the light of an admission of what has been denied in the way of being and in categories of social understanding. "To descend in order to ascend" also may be applied to the role of a sacred, apparently transcendental mediation in the process of social explanation. The way of doing or practicing social explanation now changes, moving beyond the current mode of exclusively bibliographical appropriation to an acknowledgment of practices of personal transformation as *integral* to the theorizing work process itself. In education, the sort of personal transformations represented in William Pinar's (1994) autobiographical approach to curriculum are examples of an embodied, experiential way of theorizing. Yet, personal reflexivity, even narrative self-presentation (Goodson, 1995), still does not fully accomplish the reformulation of basic categories of social explanation that a willingness to pursue premodern sacred traditions allows.

By moving out of the frame of modern, secular social science, a gate is opened to rethinking the taken-for-granted terms of social explanation. Not that escape from Western sociology is fully achievable or desirable at this stage. However, a refocusing of interest on the existential tasks set by sociocultural change and an amplifying from those subjectivities to their immediate and antecedent articulations widens not only the historical possibilities of individual-collective transformation, but also the languages that both represent collective subjective changes and anticipate and enable them. Here, for example, I have opened a reconsideration of the meaning of "presence," against the postmodern philosophical preoccupation with "absence" as an escape route from traditions of European philosophy.

This interest leads to a rethinking of social interaction that enhances or impedes presence; an understanding of sacred traditions directed toward that same question; and to a rethinking of the transformative mediating role of the sacred within social interaction. Such a sacredly transformed interaction, different but still most like Buber's I-Thou or Levinas's other, changes the meaning of experienced time, in the fullness of being, and suggests an ideal interactional mode in "cleaving" or communion. And this has implications not only for how we might understand social interactional possibilities, but also, in terms of resacralization, for educational practice.

What we are on the cusp of asking here is this: Having traced a sociocultural historical change and identified new/old cultural resources that are resonant with, but analytically richer than, the subjective present, can we also "return" to an explanatory social analysis? I have tried to offer beginning examples here. Hopefully, this is an incipient contribution, and what lies beyond it is a new cultural basis for social explanation that incites the same sort of renaissance in social theory and education that the rise of European scientific rationalism offered to the emergence of sociology. Such a new social analysis and model of educational practice is, as I have tried to show, intertwined with the evolution of the wider sociocultural system. We will have to work to simultaneously transform both the system of social practice and its rationale of social explanation.

Coda: Sacred Eros

From among possible theoretical unifications and differentiations of the "other side," the relation between the erotic and the sacred has scarcely been mentioned. Yet, in this brief catalog of social analytic work, no other relation may finally be as important. The alternative to a split between transcendent and immediate intersubjectivity can be found in retheorizing the erotic dynamics of social interaction.

We have been accustomed to accepting Freud and psychoanalytic theory as the resource for understanding attachment, separation and conflict. But the resacralizing of social theory reopens the Freudian case and the role of eros in the transformative interaction that we are calling education. David Bakan (1958) and others already have reread Freud in the palimpsest of Jewish mysticism. The future question is what such a more extensive theoretical resacralization can mean for understanding eros, interaction and education.

Song of Songs is regarded as simultaneously a biblical and kabbalist text. As the modern kabbalist, Carlo Suares (1972) argues, this poem of love and sex has been variously interpreted as an interaction of God and Israel, or, in Christianity, as the "love of Christ for his Church." Suares's kabbalist interpretation turns on a play of Hebrew letters, translating the Song of Songs as Residue of Residues or Quintessence of Quintessences.

First, the biblical verses, then, second, the kabbalist reading of this multilevel poem, in a feminine voice of a maiden of Shulam or a daughter of Jerusalem:

> Upon my bed by night I sought him whom my soul loves; I sought him but found him not; I called him but he gave no

answer. I will rise now and go about the city, in the streets and in the squares; I will seek him whom my soul loves. I sought him, but found him not.

The watchmen found me, as they went about in the city. "Have you seen him whom my soul loves" (Suares, 1972:83,84)?

I heard him, he came into me, but I am still looking for him. His breath and my body are united, yet I do not know where this union took place. His presence in me was radiance; so bright—how could I catch hold of it?

I set out to look for him among the items of my work, contradictory they turned me round and round upon myself and I did not find him.

Their energies swirled about in self-protection, closing in, pressing upon me as I went on asking: where is my love? (Suares, 1972:82,83,84).

Bibliography

Afterman, Allen. (1992). *Kabbalah and consciousness.* New York: The Sheep Meadow Press.

Alberoni, Francisco. (1984). *Movement and institution.* New York: Columbia University.

Alexander, Jeffrey C. (1988). Introduction in Jeffery Alexander (Ed.), *Durkheimian sociology cultural studies.* Cambridge: Cambridge University Press.

Anderson, Gary. (1989). Critical ethnography in education: Origins, current status and new directions. *Review of Educational Research, 59* (Fall): 249-70.

Appel, Stephen. (1992). Psychoanalysis and new sociology of education: Positioning subjects. Ph.D.diss. University of Rochester.

Apple, Michael. (1993). *Official knowledge: Democratic education in a conservative age.* New York: Routledge.

———(1979). *Ideology and curriculum.* Boston: Routledge & Kegan Paul.

———(1982). *Economic and cultural reproduction in education.* Boston: Routledge & Kegan Paul.

Arditi, Jorge. (1993). Out of the maze? Twists and riddles of postmodern thinking. *Contemporary Sociology: A Journal of Reviews* 22 : 1.

Aronowitz, Stanley. (1981). *The crisis in historical materialism: Class, politics, and culture in marxist theory.* New York: Praeger, AJF Bergin Publishers.

Aronowitz, Stanley. and Giroux, Henry. (1991). *Postmodern education.* Minneapolis: University of Minnesota Press.

———(1985). *Education under seige.* MA: Bergin & Garvey Publishers, Inc.

Bailyn, Bernard. (1960). *Education and the forming of American society: Needs and opportunities.* Williamsburg, VA: University of North Carolina Press.

Bakan, David. (1958). *Sigmund Freud and the Jewish mystical tradition.* Princeton, NJ: Van Nostrand.

Baudrillard, Jean. (1988). *Selected writings*. Edited with an introduction by Mark Poster. Stanford, CA: Stanford University Press.

Beck, Ulrich. (1992). *Risk society: Towards a new modernity.* London: Sage Publications.

Bellah, Robert (Ed.). (1973). *Emile Durkheim on morality and society.* Chicago: The University of Chicago Press.

Benjamin, Jessica. (1988). *The bonds of love: Psychoanalysis, feminism, and the problem of domination.* New York: Pantheon Books.

Bernstein, Basil. (1990). *The structuring of pedagogic discourse.* New York: Routledge.

Blackburn, Robin. (1972). *Ideology in social science: Readings in critical social theory.* New York: Pantheon Books.

Bloom, Harold. (1992). *The American religion: The emergence of the post-Christian nation.* New York: Simon and Schuster.

———(1982). *Agon: Towards a theory of revisionism.* New York: Oxford University Press.

———(1980). *A map of misreading.* New York: Oxford University Press.

———(1975). *Kabbalah and criticism.* New York: Seabury Press.

———(1973). *The anxiety of influence.* New York: Oxford University Press.

Bradley, Ann. (1992a). Pioneering board faces challenges in setting standards for teachers. *Education Week, XI* (June 3): 1.

———(1992b). N.Y.C. to create small, theme-oriented high schools. *Education Week, XI,* (April 1): 5.

Bramson, Leon. (1961). *The political context of sociology.* NJ: Princeton University Press.

Brown, Norman O. (1959). *Life against death: The psychoanalytical meaning of history.* Middletown, CT: Wesleyan University Press.

Brubaker, Rogers. (1984). *The limits of rationality: An essay on the social and moral thought of Max Weber.* London: George Allen & Unwin.

Buber, Martin. (1992). *On intersubjectivity and cultural creativity.* Edited with an introduction by S. N. Eisenstadt. Chicago: University of Chicago Press.

———(1972). *On Judaism.* Edited by Nahum N. Glatzer. New York: Schocken Books Inc.

———(1965). *Between man and man.* New York: Collier Books.

———(1974). *Pointing the way.* New York: Schocken Books.

———(1963). *Israel and the world: Essays in a time of crisis.* New York: Schocken Books.

———(1965). The education of character. An address to the National Conference of Palestinian Teachers. In Martin Buber, *Between man and man.* (104-117). New York: Collier Books.

———(1965). Education: The development of the creative powers in the child. An address to the Third International Educational Conference, Heidelberg. In Martin Buber, *Between man and man.* (83-103). New York: Collier Books.

Burwick, Frederick and Douglass, Paul (Eds.). (1992). *The crisis in modernism: Bergson and the vitalist controversy.* Cambridge: Cambridge University Press.

Callahan, Raymond E. (1962). *Education and the cult of efficiency.* Chicago: University of Chicago Press.

Callewaert, Staf. (1995). Some comments upon P. Wexler, New age sociology and education. *Studies in educational theory and curriculum. 16*:47-56.

Cascardi, Anthony J. (1992). *The subject of modernity.* New York: Cambridge University Press.

Casey, Catherine. (1995). *Work, self and society: After industrialism.* New York: Routledge.

Castoriadis, Cornelius. (1992). The retreat from autonomy: Post-modernism as generalized conformism. *Thesis Eleven.* No.31:14-24.

Chiari, Joseph. (1992). Vitalism and contemporary thought. In Burwick, Frederick and Douglass, Paul. (Eds.). *The crisis in modernism: Bergson and the vitalist controversy* (245-73). Cambridge: Cambridge University Press.

Cohen, Adir. (1983). *The educational philosophy of Martin Buber.* Teaneck: Fairleigh Dickinson University Press.

Coleman, James S. (1993). Presidential address: The rational reconstruction of society. *American Sociological Review, 58* (February):1-15.

Cremin, Lawrence A. (1961). *The transformation of the school: Progressivism in American education, 1876-1957.* New York: Alfred A. Knopf.

Csikszentmihalyi, Mihaly. (1993). *The evolving self: A psychology for the third millennium.* New York: Harper Collins Publishers.

———(1990). *Flow: The psychology of optimal experience.* New York: Harper and Row.

Deleuze, Gilles and Guattari, Felix. (1977). *Capitalism and Schizophrenia.* New York: Viking Press.

Demott, Benjamin. (1994). Morality Plays. *Harper's Magazine,* (Dec.) 289:67-76.

Dreeben, Robert. (1968). *On what is learned in school.* Menlo Park, CA: Addison-Wesley Publishing Company.

Durkheim, Emile. (1960). Preface to L'Annee Sociologique. In Kurt Wolff (Ed.). *Essays on sociology and philosophy,* (vols. 1 and 2). New York: Harper & Row, Publishers.

———(1961). *The elementary forms of the religious life.* New York: Collier Books.

Erikson, Erik. (1963). *Childhood and society.* New York: Norton.

Fauteux, Kevin. (1994). *The recovery of self: Regression and redemption in religious experience.* New York: Paulist Press.

Foss, Daniel and Larkin, Ralph. (1986). *Beyond revolution: A theory of new social movements.* South Hadley. MA: Bergan and Garvey.

Foucault, Michel. (1977). *Discipline and punishment.* New York: Pantheon.

———(1990). *The use of pleasure: Vol. 2, The history of sexuality.* New York: Vintage.

———(1982). Afterward: The subject and power. In Hubert L.Dreyfus and Paul Rabinow. *Michel Foucault: Beyond structuralism and hermeneutics.* Chicago: University of Chicago Press.

Fromm, Erich. (1964). Forward in Karl Marx, *Selected writings in sociology and social philosophy.* New York: McGraw-Hill Book Company.

———(1976). *To have or to be.* New York: Harper & Row.

———(1966). *You shall be as gods: A radical interpretation of the Old Testament and its traditions.* Greenwich: Fawcett Publications, Inc.

———(1994). *The art of being.* New York: Continuum.

———(1956). *The art of loving.* New York: Harper & Row, Publishers.

Gendlin, Eugene T. (1987). A philosophical critique of the concept of narcissism: The significance of the awareness movement in David Michael Levin (Ed.). *Pathologies of the modern self: Postmodern studies on narcissism, schizophrenia, and depression.* New York: New York University Press.

Gergen, Kenneth J. (1994). *Realities and relationships: soundings in social construction.* Cambridge, MA: Harvard University Press.

———(1991). *The saturated self: Dilemmas of identity in contemporary life.* New York: Basic Books.

Gerth, Hans Heinrich, and Mills, C. Wright (Eds.). (1946). *From Max Weber: Essays in sociology.* New York: Oxford University Press.

Geyer, Felix, and Heinz, Walter R. (Eds.). (1992). *Alienation, society, and the individual.* New Brunswick: Transaction Publishers.

Giroux, Henry. (1983). *Theory and resistance in education.* South Hadley, MA: Bergen & Garvey.

Glasser, William. (1992). Quality, trust, and redefining education. *Education Week, XI* (May 13): 34.

Glatzer, Nathan. (1953). *Franz Rosenzweig: His life and thought.* New York: Schocken Books.

Goodson, Ivor. (1995). *The making of curriculum: Collected essays.* 2nd Ed. New York: Falmer Press.

Gore, Jennifer M. (1995). Foucault's poststructuralism and observational education research: A study of power relations. In *After postmodernism: Education, politics, and identity.* (98-111). Richard Smith and Philip Wexler (Eds.). Washington, D.C.: Falmer Press.

———(1993). *The struggle for pedagogies: Critical and feminist discourses as regimes of truth.* New York: Routledge.

Gouldner, Alvin. (1970). *The coming crisis of western sociology.* New York: Basic Books.

Gover, Nathan. (1984). The educational conception implied in the psychological, humanistic and social theories of Erich Fromm. Ph.D. diss. Hebrew University.

Gutek, Gerald. (1988). *Philosophical and ideological perspectives on education.* Englewood Cliffs, NJ: Prentice Hall. Inc.

Habermas, Jurgen. (1987). *The theory of communicative action.* Boston, MA: Beacon Press.

Handelman, Susan. (1991). *Fragments of redemption: Jewish thought and literary theory in Benjamin, Scholem, and Levinas.* Bloomington: Indiana University Press.

———(1982). *The slayer of Moses: The emergence of rabbinic interpretation in modern literary theory.* Albany, NY: State University of New York Press.

Hanushek, Eric A, (et al). (1994). *Making schools work: Improving performance and controlling costs.* Washington, D.C.: The Brookings Institution.

Harp, Lonnie. (1992). Panel blueprint seeks to relate school to work. *Education Week, XI* (April 15): 1.

Harvey, David. (1989). *The condition of postmodernity.* Cambridge, MA: Basil Blackwell Inc.

Hawthorn, Geoffrey. (1976). *Enlightenment and despair: A history of sociology.* New York: Cambridge University Press.

Hinkle, Roscoe C., Jr., and Hinkle, Gisela J. (1954). *The development of modern sociology.* New York: Random House.

Hirschhorn, Larry. (1988). *The workplace within: Psychodynamics of organizational life.* Cambridge, MA: MIT Press.

Honneth, Axel. (1992). Pluralization and recognition: On the self misunderstanding of postmodern social theorists. In *Thesis eleven: Perspectives on social theory, 31*:24-33. Cambridge,. MA: MIT Press.

Horkheimer, Max, and Adorno, Theodor W. (1972). *Dialectic of enlightenment.* New York: Herder and Herder.

Hoy, David Couzens (Ed.). (1986). *Foucault: A critical reader.* From Un Cour inedit de Michel Foucault. *Magazine litteraire.* 1984 (May): 39.

Hunter, Ian. (1994). *Rethinking the school: Subjectivity, bureaucracy, criticism.* New York: St. Martin's Press.

Hunter, James Davison, and Fessenden, Tracy. (1992). The new capitalist class: The rise of the moral entrepreneur in America (United States). In Hansfried Kellner and Frank W. Heuberger, *Hidden technocrats: The new class and new capitalism:* 157-187. London: Transaction Publishers.

Idel, Moshe. (1988). *Kabbalah: New perspectives.* New Haven: Yale University Press.

James, William. (1982). *The varieties of religious experience.* New York: Penguin Books. (Original edition, 1902.)

Jay, G. and Graff, Gerald. (1993). Some questions about critical pedagogy. *Newsletter of Teachers for a Democratic Culture:* 2.

Jonas, Hans. (1974). *Philosophical essays: From ancient creed to technological man.* Englewood Cliffs, NJ: Prentice-Hall Inc.

Kaminer, Wendy. (1992). *I'm dysfunctional, you're dysfunctional: The recovery movement and other self-help fashions.* Reading, MA: Addison-Wesley.

Katz, Michael. (1971). *Class, bureaucracy and schools: The illusion of educational change in America.* New York: Praeger.

Kellner, Hansfried, and Heuberger, Frank W. (Eds.). (1992). *Hidden technocrats: The new class and new capitalism.* London: Transaction Publishers.

Kerr, John H., and Apter, Michael J. (Eds.). (1991). *Adult play: A reversal theory approach.* Amsterdam: Swets and Zeitlinger Inc.

Kimball, Bruce. (1995). Personal correspondence.

Kovel, Joel. (1991). *History and spirit: An inquiry into the philosophy of liberation.* Boston. MA: Beacon Press.

Kroker, Arthur, and Cook, David. (1986). *The postmodern scene.* New York: St. Martin's Press.

LaBier, Douglas. (1989). *Modern madness: The hidden link between work and emotional conflict.* New York: Simon and Schuster.

Langman, Lauren. (1991). From pathos to panic: American character meets the future. In Philip Wexler (Ed.), *Critical theory now:* 165-241. London: Falmer Press.

Lasch, Christopher. (1978). *The culture of narcissism: American life in an age of diminishing expectations.* New York: Norton.

Lash, Scott. (1995). Tradition and the Limits of Difference. In Paul Heelas, Scott Lash and Paul Morris (Eds.), *De-Traditionalization: Critical reflections on authority and identity:* 250-274. Cambridge, MA: Blackwell.

Levinas, Emmanuel. (1994). *Outside the subject.* Stanford, California: Stanford University Press.

———(1990). *Nine Talmudic readings.* Bloomington and Indianapolis: Indiana University Press.

Lindholm, Charles. (1990). *Charisma.* Cambridge, MA: Basil Blackwell Inc.

Lowy, Michael. (1992). *Redemption and utopia: Jewish libertarian thought in central Europe.* Stanford, CA: Stanford University Press.

Lyotard, Jean Francois. (1984). *The postmodern condition: A report on knowledge.* Minneapolis: University of Minnesota.

Mann, W. Edward and Hoffman, Edward. (1980). *Wilhelm Reich: The man who dreamed of tomorrow.* Northamptonshire: The Aquarian Press.

Marcuse, Herbert. (1964). *One-dimensional man.* Boston, Beacon Press.

———(1955). *Eros and civilization: A philosophical inquiry into Freud.* Boston: Beacon Press.

Marx, Karl. (1964). *Selected writings in sociology and social philosophy.* Edited and translated by T. B. Bottomore with introduction and notes by Maximilien Rubel. New York and London: McGraw-Hill.

———(1978). *The Marx-Engels reader.* Edited by Robert Tucker, New York: W. W. Norton.

McDermott, Robert A. (1993). Esoteric philosophy. In Robert Solomon and Kathleen Higgins (Eds.), *From Africa to zen: An invitation to world philosophy.* Boston: Rowman & Littlefield Publishers, Inc.

McGrath, Dennis, and Spear, Martin. (1991). *The academic crisis of the community college.* Albany, New York: State University of New York Press.

McLaren, Peter. (1995). *Critical pedagogy and predatory culture.* New York: Routledge.

Melucci, Alberto. (1989). *Nomads of the present: social movements and individual needs in contemporary society.* Philadelphia: Temple University Press.

Mendes-Flohr, Paul (Ed.). (1989). *From mysticism to dialogue: Martin Buber's transformation of German social thought.* Detroit: Wayne State University Press.

———(Ed.). (1988). *The philosophy of Franz Rosenzweig.* Hanover and London: University Press of New England.

Merkur, Dan. (1993). *Gnosis: An esoteric tradition of mystical visions and unions.* Albany, NY: State University of New York Press.

Mestrovic, Stjepan G. (1991). *The coming fin de siecle: An application of Durkheim's sociology to modernity and postmodernism.* New York: Routledge.

Mickelson, Roslyn A. (1996). Opportunity and danger: Understanding the business contribution to public education reform. In Kathryn Borman, Peter Cookson, Jr., Alan Sadovnick, and Joan Spade. (Eds.), *Implementing educational reform: Sociological perspectives on educational policy.* Norwood, NJ: Ablex Publishers Inc.

Mills, C. Wright. (1943). The professional ideology of social pathologists. In Larry T. Reynolds and Janice M. Reynolds (Eds.), *The Sociology of sociology:* 129-151. New York: David McKay Company, Inc.

Mongardini, Carlo. (1990). The decadence of modernity: The delusions of progress and the search for historical consciousness. In Jeffery Alexander and Piotr Sztompka (Eds.), *Rethinking Progress:* 53-66 Boston: Unwin Hyman.

Moore, Thomas. (1992). *Care of the soul.* New York: Harper Collins Publisher.

Nemiroff, Greta. (1992). *Reconstructing education: Toward a pedagogy of critical humanism.* New York: Bergin and Garvey.

Noble, Douglas. (1996). Selling schools a bill of goods: The marketing of computer-based education. *Afterimage, 5.* (March/April): 13-19.

———(1991). *The classroom arsenal: Military research, information technology, and public education.* London: Falmer Press.

Olalquiaga, Celeste. (1992). *Megalopolis: Contemporary cultural sensibilities.* Minneapolis, MN: University of Minnesota Press.

Ollman, Bertell. (1971). *Alienation: Marx's conception of man in capitalist society.* Cambridge: Cambridge University Press.

O'Neill, John. (1986). Sociological nemesis: Parsons and Foucault on the therapeutic disciplines. In Mark L. Wardell and Stephen P. Turner (Eds.), *Sociological theory in transition:* 21-35 Boston: Allen & Unwin.

Panitch, Leo. (1977). The development of corporatism in liberal democracies. *Comparative Political Studies, 10:* 61-90.

Parsons, Talcott. (1961). The school class as a social system. In A.H. Halsey. Jean Floud and C. Arnold Anderson (Eds.), *Education, economy, and society: A reader in the sociology of education:* 434-455 New York: The Free Press.

———(1955). *Family, socialization, and interaction process.* Glencoe: Free Press.

Passmore, John. (1980). *The philosophy of teaching.* Cambridge, MA: Harvard University Press.

Perkinson, Henry. (1993). *Teachers without goals: Students without purposes.* New York: McGraw-Hill.

Pinar, William. (1994). *Autobiography, politics and sexuality: Essays in curriculum theory 1972-1992.* New York: P. Lang.

Ray, B., and Mickelson, R. (1989). Business leaders and the politics of school reforms. *Yearbook of the Politics of Education Association.* New York: Falmer Press.

Reich, Wilhelm. (1971). *The mass psychology of fascism.* New York: Farrar, Straus, & Giroux.

———(1961). *The Function of the orgasm.* New York: Farrar, Straus, and Giroux.

———(1949). *Character analysis.* New York: Farrar, Straus, & Giroux.

———(1972). *Sex-Pol.* New York: Vintage.

———(1980). *Genitality in the theory and therapy of the neuroses.* New York: Farrar, Straus, & Giroux.

Reisby, Kirsten, and Schnack, Karsten. (1995). *What can curriculum studies and pedagogy learn from sociology today?* Copenhagen, Denmark: Royal Danish School of Educational Studies

Roberts, S. (1994). When government plays entrepreneur. *The New York Times,* Dec.11: section 4, 1. New York.

Roof, Wade. (1993). *A generation of seekers: The spiritual journeys of the baby boom generation.* New York: HarperCollins Publishers.

Sadovnik, Alan. (1995). *Knowledge and pedagogy: The sociology of Basil Bernstein.* Norwood, NJ: Ablex Publishing Corporation.

Schmoker, Mike. (1992). What schools can learn from Toyota America. *Education Week, XI,* May 13: 23.

Schneider, Michael. (1975). *Neurosis of civilization: A Marxist/Freudian synthesis*. New York: Seabury.

Scholem, Gershom. (1971). *The messianic idea in Judaism*. New York: Schocken Books.

———(1991). *On the mystical shape of the godhead*. New York: Schocken Books, Inc.

———(1974). *Major trends in Jewish mysticism*. New York: Schocken Books.

Schwendinger, Herman, and Schwendinger, Julia R. (1974). *The sociologists of the chair: A radical analysis of the formative years of North American sociology, 1883-1922*. New York: Basic Books.

Seidman, Steven. (1991). The end of sociological theory: The postmodern hope. *Sociological Theory*, Vol.9. American Sociological Association, Blackwell.

Shakolsky, Leon. (1970). The development of sociological theory in America—A sociology of knowledge interpretation. In Larry T. Reynolds and Janice M. Reynolds. (Eds.), *The Sociology of sociology*: 6-30. New York: David McKay Company, Inc.

Singh, Parlo. (1995). Voicing the 'other,' speaking for the 'self,' disrupting the metanarratives of educational theorizing with poststructural feminisms. In Richard Smith and Philip Wexler (Eds.), *After postmodernism: education, politics, and identity*: 182-206. Washington, D.C.: Falmer Press.

Slater, Philip. (1980). *Wealth addiction*. New York: Nutton.

Slaughter, Sheila. (1975). Ph.D. diss. University of Wisconson at Madison.

Smith, Dusky Lee. (1970). Sociology and the rise of corporate capitalism. In Larry T. Reynolds and Janice M. Reynolds (Eds.),. *The Sociology of sociology*: 371-387. New York: David McKay Company, Inc.

Smith, Richard, and Wexler, Philip. (1995). *After postmodernism: Education, politics and identity*. Washington, D.C.: Falmer Press.

Sommerfield, M. (1992). National commitment to parent role in schools sought. *Education Week, XI*, April 15: 1.

Sorokin, Pitirim. (1957). *Social and cultural dynamics: A study of change in major systems of art, truth, ethics, law and social relationships*. Boston: Porter Sargent Publisher.

Steinsaltz, Adin. (1992). *In the beginning: Discourses on Chasidic thought*. Northvale, NJ: Jason Aronson, Inc.

Suares, Carlo. (1972). *The Song of songs*. Berkeley and London: Shambala.

Sullivan, Edmund. (1990). *Critical psychology and pedagogy: Interpretation of the personal world.* New York: Bergin & Garvey Publishers.

Sunker, Heinz. (1994). *Pedagogy, politics and democracy.* Germany: University of Wupperal.

Thompson, Kenneth. (1990). Secularization and sacralization. In *Rethinking progress: Movements, forces, and ideas at the end of the 20th century.* Boston: Unwin Hyman.

Touraine, Alain. (1988). *Return of the actor: Social theory in postindustrial society.* Minneapolis: University of Minnesota Press.

Tucker, Marc S. (1992). The roundtable: A new 'social compact' for mastery in education. *Education Week,* June 17: S3-S5.

Viadero, D. (1992). Maine's 'common core' offers a lesson in standards. *Education Week, XI,* April 15: 21.

Vidich, A. J., and Lyman, Stanford. (1986). State, ethics and public morality in American sociological thought. In M. Wardell and S. Turner (Eds.), *Sociological Theory in Transition.* Boston: Allen & Unwin.

———(1985). *American sociology.* New Haven and London: Yale University Press.

Vincent, Jean-Marie. (1991). *Abstract labour: A critique.* New York: St Martin's Press.

Weber, Max. (1968). *Economy and society.* New York: Bedminster Press.

———(1963). *The sociology of religion.* Boston: Beacon Press.

———(1958). *The protestant ethic and the spirit of capitalism.* New York: Charles Scribner's Sons.

———(1946). *From Max Weber: Essays in sociology.* Translated, edited, and with an introduction by H.H. Gerth and C. Wright Mills. New York: Oxford University Press.

Weinstein, James. (1968). *The corporate ideal in the liberal state, 1900-1918.* Boston: Beacon Press.

Welter, Rick. (1962). *Popular education and democratic thought in America.* New York: Columbia University.

Wexler, Philip. (In preparation). Quantum sociology: Social theory and education in a new age.

———(in press) Alienation, new age sociology and the Jewish way. In Felix Geyer (Ed.), *Alienation, ethnicity and postmodernism.*

———(1995) Bernstein: A Jewish misreading. In Alan Sadovnik (Ed.), *Knowledge and pedagogy: The sociology of Basil Bernstein: 111-123.* Norwood, NJ: Ablex Publishing Co.

———(1993/94). Educational corporatism and its counterposes. *Arena Journal,* no. 2: 175-194.

———(1992). *Becoming somebody: Toward a social psychology of school.* Washington, D.C.: Falmer Press.

———(1991). *Critical theory now.* New York and Philadelphia: Falmer Press.

———(1987). *Social analysis of education: After the new sociology.* New York: Routledge, Chapman and Hall, Inc.

———(1983). *Critical social psychology.* Boston and London: Routledge and Kegan Paul.

———(1976). *The sociology of education: Beyond equality.* Indianapolis: Bobbs-Merrill.

———(1972). Children of the immigrants: A study of education, ethnicity and social change in Israel. Ph.D. Diss. Princeton University.

Wexler, Philip, and Grabiner, G. (1985). The education question: America during the crisis. In R. Sharp (Ed.), *Capitalist crisis, education and the state: A comparative politics of education.* Melbourne: Macmillan.

Whimster, Sam, and Scott Lash (Eds.). (1987). *Max Weber, rationality and modernity.* London: Allen.

Wolk, R. (Ed.). (1992). A new 'social compact' for mastery in education. *Education Week, XI,* June 17: 4.

Wrigley, Julia. (1982). *Class politics and public schools: Chicago, 1900-1950.* New Brunswick, NJ: Rutgers University Press.

Wuthnow, Robert. (1992). *Rediscovering the sacred.* Michigan: William B. Eerdmans Publishing Company.

Yuasa, Yasuo. (1993). *The body, self-cultivation, and ki-energy.* Albany, NY: State University of New York Press.

Index